OUR HOLY FAITH
A RELIGION SERIES for THE ELEMENTARY SCHOOLS

TEACHER'S MANUAL for

Living Like Christ, In Christ

✝ ✝
✝ ✝ ✝

Based on the second half of the
No. 1 Revised Baltimore Catechism
(Confraternity Edition)

ST. AUGUSTINE ACADEMY PRESS
HOMER GLEN, ILLINOIS

Nihil obstat:
    JOHN F. MURPHY, S.T.D.
    Censor librorum

Imprimatur:
    + WILLIAM E. COUSINS
    Archiepiscopus Milwauchiensis
    September 16, 1960

This book was originally published in 1960
by Bruce Publishing, Milwaukee.

CONTENTS

GENERAL INTRODUCTION FOR THE SERIES

OUR HOLY FAITH

The Series, OUR HOLY FAITH, is intended to provide a complete, integrated, and basic course in religion for the eight grades of the elementary school.

The purpose of. teaching religion in the elementary school is to see to it that the pupil has a clear and adequate knowledge of his holy Faith, so as to guide and influence his will to use grace in forming the image of Christ in himself. While primarily addressed to the intellect, it does not neglect the will or the child's attitudes and emotions. The first purpose of this religion Series, therefore, is clear and adequate knowledge of the Catholic religion.

The psychological basis for this is to be found in St. Augustine's little gem, "On Catechizing the Unlettered."*

St. Augustine tells us that in teaching religion we must lead the pupil from faith, to hope, to charity. The first step, therefore, is knowledge of our religion based on supernatural faith. The child is taught and accepts what Christ's Church, through her representative, proposes to be believed.

Content and Arrangement of the Series — Grades 1 and 2

The content of the first two grades is the traditional content of those grades, with emphasis on Confession and Holy Communion in the second grade.

Grades 3, 4, and 5

The first two grades are followed by two cycles of three grades each — 3 to 5 and 6 to 8. In Grades 3, 4, and 5, the No. 1 Baltimore Catechism is followed in the exact sequence of its lessons and indeed of its questions, in such fashion, however, that the first half of the No. 1 Revised Baltimore Catechism** (the Creed and the first three Commandments) is covered in the first book of that sequence (GOD'S TRUTHS HELP US LIVE); the second half of the No. 1 Catechism is covered in the third book of that sequence (LIVING LIKE CHRIST IN CHRIST). The second book of that sequence (THE VINE AND THE BRANCHES) is devoted to a study of the liturgy and the liturgical year. In this book the catechetical approach is, for obvious reasons, omitted. We have placed this material, which deals with an impor-

tant area of religious instruction omitted in the Catechism, between two books devoted to explaining the Catechism.

Thus, the suggested sequence for Grades 3 to 5 is:

Grade 3 — GOD'S TRUTHS HELP US LIVE
(First half of No. 1 Catechism)

Grade 4 — THE VINE AND THE BRANCHES
(The liturgy and the liturgical year)

Grade 5 — LIVING LIKE CHRIST IN CHRIST
(Second half of No. 1 Catechism)

One value of this sequence is that it provides an alternation from the Catechism, applying the same doctrines but in a completely different manner.

Grades 6, 7, and 8

The books for the three remaining grades — 6, 7, and 8 — are similarly organized. In the first book of the sequence, OUR FAITH: GOD'S GREAT GIFT, the pupil studies the first half of the No. 2 Revised Baltimore Catechism. The second half of the No. 2 Catechism is then taken up in the volume, TO LIVE IS CHRIST, which is recommended for Grade 8 because it contains a review of the first half of the No. 2 Catechism and an intense study of its second half. The third book in this sequence (recommended for Grade 7, but usable in any grade from the sixth to the eighth) is entitled CHRIST: IN PROPHECY, IN PERSON, AND IN HIS CHURCH. It contains a complete chronological treatment of Bible History and of Church History, which have often been neglected in recent courses of study. The suggested sequence for Grades 6 to 8 is this:

Grade 6 — OUR FAITH: GOD'S GREAT GIFT
(First half of No. 2 Catechism)

Grade 7 — CHRIST: IN PROPHECY, IN PERSON, AND IN HIS CHURCH
(Bible History — Church History)

Grade 8 — TO LIVE IS CHRIST
(Second half of No. 2 Catechism)

Flexibility of the Series

Although the Series follows the sequence of the Catechism, its subject matter is so arranged that it is pos-

---

* There are many translations; that of Rev. Joseph P. Christopher, *De catechizandis Rudibus* (Washington, D. C.: Catholic University, 1926), is very good.

** All references to the Catechism are to the Confraternity Edition.

sible for a superintendent, a pastor, or a principal to adapt it to almost every course of study for religion in the elementary grades, or vice versa, to adapt the course of study to fit the Series. Since it contains books that are devoted to a study of the liturgy and of biblical and Church history, the Series makes it possible for the teacher to break up the monotony that frequently results from studying nothing but the Catechism year after year.

It is suggested that the book covering the first half of the No. 1 Catechism be used in Grade 3 and that the one dealing with the second half be employed for Grade 5, with the book on the liturgy for Grade 4. However the order of sequence can be changed if another order seems more appropriate. The book on the liturgy, THE VINE AND THE BRANCHES, can be postponed to Grade 5 if it is thought too difficult for Grade 4 (it is, however, no more difficult than science or geography in that grade); or it can be anticipated in an earlier grade or even completely omitted. The latter possibility, however, is one which the authors hope is not considered. Our present courses of study in elementary religion almost universally omit an ordered and intensive study of the liturgy and the liturgical year, which, as Pope Pius XII reminded us, is a basic means of religious instruction.

Method of Handling the Catechism

In the past, the method of teaching religion in the elementary schools was, quite justly, criticized for its misuse of the Catechism. The fault certainly did not lie in the Catechism, which is intended as a concise and precise synopsis of religious knowledge. The Catechism is designed to be studied carefully *after* it has been taught and explained authoritatively in the name of the Church.

Too often, however, the authoritative teaching and presentation have been omitted, and the child has been led directly to the bald, synoptic questions and answers of the Catechism, which he has been directed to study before or without any explanation and then repeat in rote fashion after he has memorized them.

Fortunately, in most modern courses of study in religion this abuse has been eliminated. The result has been courses of study more enjoyable to teacher and pupil alike.

Unfortunately, in many instances, the Catechism has also been abandoned. Bishops and pastors have deplored this, with great justification. An ordered knowledge of one's religion is absolutely necessary, and this the Catechism insures.

In this Series we have retained the exact sequence of the Catechisms No. 1 and No. 2. However, we have taken care to teach the content of the lessons *before* asking the child to study and, if needed, to memorize the Catechism questions and answers. Thus we hope we have met the reasonable desires of the clergy, by accenting the Catechism, while not forgetting the needs and problems of the pupils and teachers in the classroom.

In many instances, while following the Catechism, we have added points not covered in it, but necessary either as matters of knowledge or as material aiding assimilation and application of the basic doctrines. Our intention has been to make the study of religion as attractive and enjoyable and instructive as possible. In short, we believe that a child's attitude toward religion is as important as his knowledge. One without the other is not of much value, and in this Series we have sought to integrate the two.

In this connection, however, let it be clearly stated and understood that the child's inclination or enjoyment is not the prime factor to be considered. We are dealing here with a matter that is not subject to the likes or dislikes of the pupil. Here we are concernd with a divinely constituted body of knowledge which the Church has a mandate to convey to the human race, and particularly to her members, in an authoritative way. "As the Father hath sent me, I also send you. Going therefore . . ." (Mt. 28:28).

Here, a curriculum solely determined by child interest or enjoyment would be an absurdity.

A Key Point — The Answer Before the Question

In the four years in which the texts of the Series are based directly on the Catechism — Grades 3, 5, 6, and 8 — we have included the Catechism answers in the body of the lessons, using the exact words of the Catechism; but we have expanded, paraphrased, and otherwise explained the meaning of the Catechism; this will insure that the child understands what the Catechism means, and will assist him to learn it when he studies the Catechism questions and answers at the end of the lesson. *The Catechism answers have been placed in boldface or in italics* to call attention to them. Thus, we teach the answer before we ask the child to learn it. The result is *understanding*, not mere rote memorization.

BASIC PRINCIPLES IN TEACHING RELIGION

What follows are the essential and fundamental principles for the teaching of religion. All else is accidental.

Begin With Faith

The first objective of the teaching of religion is a knowledge of the truths God wants us to know, and an acceptance of those truths on the basis of God's veracity —namely, an informed but unhesitating faith.

End With Love

The supreme objective of the teaching of religion, however, is not faith but love — love of God. The objective we have had in building this Series, and the objective the teachers of religion must have in teaching it, is to lead the pupil to a supernatural love of God.

With St. Augustine we ask every teacher of this Series to refer everything she teaches to the love of God — God's love for us as proved by what He has done for us, and our love of God as proved by how we serve God in Himself and in our neighbors.

With God's love for us and ours for Him ever in

mind, the teacher should present the doctrines and moral precepts of the Catholic religion in such a fashion that they lead the child first to an appreciation of his faith and a strengthening of that virtue in him; then to an increase of hope in him, for without supernatural hope there will be no continued striving.

The end, however, is love. The pupil should be led to see in everything that God has done an evidence of His love for us. He has loved us enough to reveal to us what He wants us to believe. He has revealed His existence, the incarnation, the redemption, the Church, the sacraments, the moral code we follow, the rewards He has in store for us, and so many other matters. In each of these truths He is proving His love for us. They should be so taught that, in all, God's love of us may stand out and arouse a desire to return love for love.

If truths are so taught, it will be easy for the child to see his obligation to love and serve God in return. They will not then be merely abstract truths with little personal meaning, but will become knowledge charged with motives for the will to requite that divine love.

Method and Content Intertwined

From the above it will be seen that method and content in the proper teaching of religion are closely intertwined. The point to be learned is first presented to the intellect as an object of faith and knowledge, then related to hope, as being possible, and finally to love as being something to be desired and possessed. All other details of methodology should be subordinated to this basic sequence.

It is all the more necessary to insist on this because the unit method we have used is also commonly employed in teaching the social studies. There, however, it is not based on supernatural virtues, but on the natural intellectual virtues.

Christian Formation

The formation of the perfect Christian, whose life is patterned on the life of Christ, is our final goal. This cannot be achieved by teaching or by the school. It is a supernatural task, requiring supernatural means. These means are in the possession of the Church. All the teacher can do is instruct and influence the pupil to fulfill his destiny as a member of Christ's Mystical Body, to see his role in the sacrifice it offers to the heavenly Father, to utilize the channels of grace it brings him. Solid, accurate, and full instruction by the teacher means much, but it does not guarantee the co-operation of the student. He still has his free will. The teacher can instruct, give good example, and pray — in doing these she does much. The home, too, can do much. But the grace of God, the Church and her means of grace, and the free will of the individual are all-important. We must do our utmost to enlighten the intellect and train the will of our charges — then leave the rest to God.

INTRODUCTION FOR TEACHER'S MANUAL TO ACCOMPANY
LIVING LIKE CHRIST, IN CHRIST

This Manual has been prepared to accompany the textbook, LIVING LIKE CHRIST, IN CHRIST, which is recommended for Grade 5, a text based on the second half of the Number 1 Baltimore Catechism (Confraternity edition). The subject matter has been divided into five units:

Unit I: THE CHIEF TRUTHS OF OUR FAITH
         (a Review)

Unit II: THE LAST SEVEN COMMANDMENTS OF
          GOD, LOVE OF NEIGHBOR

Unit III: THE COMMANDMENTS OF THE CHURCH

Unit IV: THE SEVEN SACRAMENTS

Unit V: SACRAMENTALS AND PRAYER

Unit I: The Chief Truths of Our Faith, is a review of the Apostles' Creed and the first three Commandments of God. Chapter 1 recalls the content of the first fourteen lessons of the Catechism on the Creed, while Chapter 2 continues the review by covering lessons 15 to 18 inclusive, which treat of the first three Commandments of God.

Unit II: The Last Seven Commandments of God, Love of Neighbor. Each of these seven Commandments is treated in a separate chapter of this unit, built around Catechism lessons 19 and 20.

Unit III: The Commandments of the Church, is a detailed explanation of Catechism lessons 21 and 22. The first chapter deals with the Commandments of the Church in general; the remaining five pertain to each of them in particular, with the exception of the third and fourth commandments, which have been combined into one chapter.

Unit IV: The Seven Sacraments, is a study of Catechism lessons 23 to 35. The first of the ten chapters in this unit is devoted to the sacraments as a means of grace. In the following chapters, each of the sacraments is given a special study. *The Mass, the Perfect Sacrifice* constitutes a chapter by itself and follows the study of the Holy Eucharist.

Unit V: Sacramentals and Prayer, contains two chapters. The first is devoted to an explanation of Catechism lesson 36 and to the study of the sacramentals most commonly used as a further means of grace. The second, *Prayer: Lifting Our Minds and Hearts to God,* is an exposition of the information presented in lesson 37.

NOTE: Certain changes have been made in this manual in accordance with the recent papal decree on the rubrics.

ARRANGEMENT OF TEACHER'S MANUAL

This Teacher's Manual begins by offering *Sample Lesson Plans* for the various types of lessons. This is followed by sections dealing with each unit of the textbook. Each section has been prepared according to the following outline:

I. OBJECTIVES OF THE UNIT

These are general in nature and may be used as a basis for the specific objectives which the individual teacher believes may best meet the needs of her class.

II. TEACHER PRESENTATION OF THE UNIT

The ideas proposed under this heading are merely suggestions, guides for classroom use. The teacher's personal experience may possibly yield other valuable ideas. The unit method is advised. The lesson types listed below are suggested for the unit method. Some of these require only one class period, whereas others may require more than one.

Specific Lesson Types (for Sample Lesson Plans exemplifying these types, cf. pp. 9–12).

The unit procedure consists of four *major* lesson types: (1) *Launching*, (2) *Study-Work*, (3) *Culmination*, and (4) *Evaluation*. Of these, the Study-Work type is subdivided into (*a*) the Development Lesson, (*b*) the Study Lesson, (*c*) the Discussion Lesson, (*d*) the Appreciation Lesson, and (*e*) the Drill Lesson. Each of these lesson types is developed according to procedures proper to it.

1. Launching

The launching lesson includes an oral or written pretest from which the teacher may determine the present knowledge of her class about the new unit. It also presents an overview of the entire unit, designed to help the teacher stress the main themes and problems of the unit, arouse interest, and challenge the pupil. Slides, filmstrips, pictures, charts, chalk talks, and other visual aids are invaluable to this particular phase of the unit.

2. Study-Work

The study-work lesson, as noted above, includes a number of subdivisions. Each of these entails a maximum of guided self-activity on the part of the pupil, and requires the teacher to develop new content matter, and to direct and inspire the child in his efforts to know, love, and serve his Creator.

a) **The Development Lesson:** The development lesson usually opens the Study-Work step. Here the teacher leads the pupil to some new understanding or knowledge by direct exposition, explanation, and discussion.

b) **The Study Lesson:** The study lesson has various procedures, but it is always intended to further or increase an understanding of the material presented in the development lesson. The study involved may be *independent individual study* or *teacher-directed study*.

c) **The Discussion Lesson:** The discussion lesson always follows a study lesson, unless the study lesson is teacher-directed. In the latter case, the discussion is a part of the study lesson. The children, under the careful guidance of the teacher, share their findings from the previous study lesson with the other members of the class. The initiative of the teacher and the previous experience of the children in participating in discussion lessons will determine the type and variety of material presented in the discussion.

d) **The Appreciation Lesson:** Although an appreciation of our faith is the keynote of every religion lesson, there is a definite need to give explicit attention to appreciation during each unit. This lesson takes on the form of a meditation resulting in some simple, yet definite and practical, resolution.

e) **The Drill Lesson:** The drill lesson is employed when a topic or section of content has been covered. Its purpose is to fix the knowledge gained thus far in the study. Here again, variety is most important in order to prevent tedium and monotony.

3. The Culmination

The culmination lesson is the organization, unification, application, and conclusion of an entire *unit* of work. The culmination activity, although designated as the third major step of the unit, is not an isolated block of work, but is the natural outcome of the study-work periods. The culmination step is best carried out if it shows how the truths of religion are correlated with other school subjects and with life.

4. The Evaluation

The ultimate aim of religious education is the formation of true and perfect Christians. Since this can be known only by God, it is apparent that the teacher cannot measure the final outcomes. However, the evaluation step is a measure of achievement, both of teacher and pupils, in so far as this is possible. A written examination and a discussion of outcomes in the light of original objectives will give evidence of the knowledge, appreciation, and attitudes acquired by the children and will also reveal weaknesses and defects in the teaching process.

Enrichment Reading: Although this is not an actual part of the unit procedure, it has its place in the teaching of religion and can be worked into either the study-work periods or possibly into the culminating activity. Books can provide material for a more active participation in the religion lesson. They offer not only information but inspiration and enrichment as well. Through them, the reader extends his knowledge beyond the mere requirements and is inspired to draw from his readings Christlike principles which become a part of his daily living.

III. OUTLINE OF SUBJECT MATTER OF THE UNIT

Here will be found a chapter-by-chapter outline for the unit.

IV. ANSWER KEY TO END-UNIT TESTS IN TEXTBOOK

V. SUGGESTED ACTIVITIES FOR UNIT

These activities represent many more activities than will likely be utilized during the unit. The individual teacher may select and use those which she feels will best suit her needs. These activities may further be used in the culmination lesson which concludes a particular unit of study.

VI. BIBLIOGRAPHY: Teacher and Pupil

VII. INSTRUCTIONAL AIDS TO BE USED BY THE TEACHER

These again may perhaps be more numerous than a teacher will find available in a given school. These aids are listed for the purpose of making known what materials may be obtained.

SAMPLE LESSON PLANS

The following sample lesson plans are suggested for each of the lesson types just enumerated. They are based on specific subject matter in the textbook, as their titles indicate. The plans apply to one particular phase of each unit. They may be used as a guide for planning similar lesson types.

I. SAMPLE LESSON PLAN FOR LAUNCHING LESSON

UNIT I: The Chief Truths of Our Faith

SUBJECT: The Apostles' Creed (review)

TYPE: Launching

OBJECTIVES:

Teacher:
A. To challenge the students to recall their previous knowledge of the Apostles' Creed.
B. To make them realize the need to review this knowledge.

Pupil:
A. To accept the challenge to recall what has already been studied.
B. To increase their understanding of the Apostles' Creed by reviewing previous knowledge.

PROCEDURE:

Approach: Direct children to observe the symbols of the twelve articles of the Creed displayed on the bulletin board.

Presentation: Call special attention to the captions and discuss each briefly.

Explanation: Direct children to the textbook. Skim pages 12–48. Read each of the section titles printed throughout these pages. Use each caption as a challenge to recall quickly important facts pertaining to it. (Failure on the part of children to remember this knowledge probably indicates the need for further study and should be treated in this manner.)

Generalization: List on the board those items in which children were weak. Draw from them a desire to use their books during future religion periods to recall what they have forgotten or to learn what they failed to learn in their previous study.

Application: Page 14 — For Me To Do: Say this prayer together (The Apostles' Creed). Think for a minute about how you can live this prayer today.

II. SAMPLE LESSON PLANS FOR STUDY-WORK LESSON

A. Development Lesson

UNIT II: The Fourth Commandment: Honor thy father and thy mother.

SUBJECT: What Is Commanded by the Fourth Commandment?

TYPE: Study-Work: Development

OBJECTIVES:

A. To increase an understanding of the Fourth Commandment.

B. To increase our knowledge of what we must do to keep the Fourth Commandment.

PROCEDURE:

Approach: Display a large illustration of the "Finding of Jesus in the Temple."

Presentation: Recall the story of the Finding of Jesus in the Temple.

Explanation: Write on the board: "What the Fourth Commandment Commands."

Have the children discuss briefly what this is.

Refer to the text, pp. 62–71. Direct the children to find the five points presented in the text which will answer the question on the blackboard.

List these points on the board and develop their meaning.

Summary: Help the children to realize that the Fourth Commandment requires us:

1. To respect our parents because they take God's place on earth.
2. To love our parents for all they do for us.
3. To obey our parents because they make known to us God's will.
4. To help our parents in order to show them how grateful we are for what they do for us.
5. To obey our lawful superiors or those who have been appointed to guide and protect us.

Application: Direct children to the suggestions on page 72: For Me To Do: Choose one you will try to do today. During the next minute meditate on this matter and pray for God's help to carry out your resolution.

B. Directed Study Lesson

UNIT II: The Last Seven Commandments of God

SUBJECT: Thou shalt not covet thy neighbor's wife.

TYPE: Study-Work: Directed Study

OBJECTIVES:

A. To develop an understanding of the Ninth Commandment of God.

B. To gain a better knowledge of what this law commands.

PROCEDURE:

Approach: Recall a few of the saints who were noted for their great love of purity.

Presentation: God loved purity so greatly that He devoted two of His laws to the practice of this virtue; e.g., the sixth and ninth.

Directed Study: Refer to text, pages 103–104.

Read the first three paragraphs. How are the Sixth and Ninth Commandments alike?

How do they differ?

Why must we be careful of our thoughts and desires?

Read the section on "Purity of Thought." Be prepared to tell how Veronica's thoughts and desires influenced her actions.

Page 104. Be ready to discuss the supernatural and natural helps to purity.

Read page 105. What special title has been given to St. Thomas Aquinas?

Why should we pray to St. Thomas Aquinas to help us in the practice of purity?

Summary: The Ninth Commandment commands us to practice purity in thought and desire.

Our thoughts and desires control our actions.

If we are pure in thought and desire, we will be pure in our actions.

Prayer and the sacraments are supernatural helps to purity.

Worthwhile activities and hobbies are natural helps to purity.

Application: Think for a minute of the many saints to whom we may pray for the virtue of purity. Ask children to name some of them. Choose one to whom you will pray especially today for this particular intention.

C. Independent Study Lesson

UNIT III: The Commandments of the Church

SUBJECT: The Holydays of Obligation

TYPE: Study-Work: Independent Study

OBJECTIVES:

A. To further an understanding of the six holydays of obligation.

B. To foster greater love of these important feasts of the Church.

PROCEDURE:

Approach: Display illustrations of the holydays of obligation. Discuss each briefly.

Presentation: Challenge children to gather more information about these feasts.

Explanation: Divide class into six groups.
Assign a holyday to each group.
Refer to study questions on the board.
Who is honored by this feast?
What event is being celebrated?
Mention any other significant information you found in your reading.
Recall standards for a worthwhile study period.
Work quietly.
Take notes that you understand.
Take notes neatly.
Use text thoroughly.
Use other reference materials.
Direct children to work independently.
Be available to assist where needed.

Application: Think for a minute about the holyday you have studied. Consider how this feast has helped you. Thank God for this blessing.

D. Discussion Lesson

UNIT III: The Commandments of the Church

SUBJECT: The Holydays of Obligation

TYPE: Study-Work: Discussion

OBJECTIVES:

A. To further the ability to take an active part in a discussion.
B. To share our findings with the members of our class through discussion.

PROCEDURE:

Approach: Arouse in children a desire to discuss the information they gathered in yesterday's study lesson.

Presentation: Draw from children the names and dates of the holydays of obligation. List them on the board.

Explanation: Recall the standards for discussion:
Take part.
Be courteous.
Speak clearly.
Appoint discussion leader for each group.
Introduce Group I: Leader states problem and proceeds with discussion based on the three points of previous day's study.
Leader may ask members of the class to summarize their discussion in one or two good statements.
Group leader may write these on the board or he may ask the child who contributed the summary statement to write it on the board.
Each group continues in this manner.

Summary: Individuals may read the summary statements from the board.

Application: We are obliged to assist at Mass on the six holydays of obligation we discussed today. We may pause for a moment now to renew our Morning Offering in which we united ourselves with the Holy Sacrifice of the Mass throughout the world. Tell God this in your own words.

E. Appreciation Lesson

UNIT IV: The Seven Sacraments

SUBJECT: Confirmation: Soldiers of Christ

TYPE: Study-Work: Appreciation

OBJECTIVES:

A. To incite a deeper appreciation of the sacrament of Confirmation.
B. To consider the blessings received in this sacrament and to express our gratitude for them.

PROCEDURE:

Reflection: Display a large illustration of the Descent of the Holy Ghost on the Apostles.
Discuss the setting, the background, and the reason for the Apostles being there.

Affections: Invite the children to imagine that they are Apostles. Present possible thoughts which an apostle might have had as he waited during the nine days and nights.
Incite children to similar considerations.
Recall with children the effects the Apostles experienced after they received the Holy Ghost.

Resolutions: Lead children to consider the fact that they, too, have received the Holy Ghost in Baptism. Think further, that in Confirmation the Holy Ghost comes to them again to increase and strengthen the gifts He gave in Baptism.
Challenge children with the question: What can I do today to show that I, like the Apostles, have received the Holy Ghost?
Conclude with the Prayer to the Holy Ghost, Text, page 165.

F. Drill Lesson

UNIT IV: The Seven Sacraments

SUBJECT: Holy Mass: The Perfect Sacrifice

TYPE: Study-Work: Drill

OBJECTIVES:

A. To provide drill for children to strengthen their knowledge of the Mass.

B. To increase mastery and retention of information gained through the study of the Mass.

PROCEDURE:

Approach: Present the challenge of a contest:
Boys *vs.* girls. Which team will win the Religion Pennant?

Devices prepared by the teacher:
Yes-No Statements
Split Sentences (Cause and effect)
Matching Terms and Definitions
Quiz Questions (to be answered in complete statements)

Evaluation:
Determine the score attained for each part of the contest, considering each device as one part.
Determine the total score and award the pennant to the winning team.

Application:
Lead children to the understanding that knowledge is not gained only for the sake of knowing more. Our increased knowledge of the Mass should incite us to an increased love for the Mass. Resolve to assist at Mass with greater attention, reverence, and love.

III. SAMPLE LESSON PLAN FOR CULMINATION LESSON

UNIT IV: The Seven Sacraments

SUBJECT: Penance: Love and Mercy

TYPE: Culmination

OBJECTIVES:

A. To provide opportunity for using the activities of this unit in a unified project.

B. To organize the activities of this topic, which resulted from initiative and originality, into a unified closing of this study.

PROCEDURE:

Approach: Propose the idea of organizing the various activities carried on during this study to form a unified culmination of the entire topic.

Presentation: Draw from children a discussion of the different activities enjoyed during this study. List them on the board.

Organization:
Sing: The Sign of the Cross; Our Father.
Dramatization of the Prodigal Son.
Illustrations depicting the five things necessary for a good confession.
Panel discussion on the subject of indulgences.
Conclusion: Hymn: God of Mercy and Compassion.

IV. SAMPLE LESSON PLAN FOR EVALUATION LESSON

UNIT V: Sacramentals and Prayer

SUBJECT: Sacramentals and Prayer

TYPE: Evaluation

OBJECTIVES:

A. To determine how well the students understand the material.

B. To evaluate the students' mastery of this study of prayer.

PROCEDURE:

Approach: Challenge class with the caption on page 264.

Presentation: Refer to the test on page 264.

Explanation: Allow time for children to scan each part of the test.
Clarify any part that presents a problem.
Call attention to the note in parentheses. Use another sheet of paper.
Direct children to read and think carefully before writing an answer.
Supervise as children work independently.
Analyze results and go over them with class.
Re-teach what was not learned or improperly conceived or poorly grasped.

Application: Refer to suggestions under *For Me To Do* on pp. 257 and 263. Which one of these would you like to do today? Ask God to help you keep your resolution.

UNIT I: *THE CHIEF TRUTHS OF OUR FAITH* (A Review Unit)

(Text, *Living Like Christ, in Christ*, pp. 11–59)

I. OBJECTIVES

A. To recall the chief truths of our faith through a brief review of the Apostles' Creed.

B. To increase our understanding of God the Father, our Creator.

C. To deepen our appreciation for God the Son, our Redeemer.

D. To strengthen our devotion to God the Holy Ghost, our Sanctifier.

E. To further the understanding that, as members of the Church, we are united to Christ and through Him to one another.

F. To increase our knowledge of the first three Commandments of God.

II. TEACHER PRESENTATION OF UNIT I

This unit, since it is a review of previous knowledge, need not be developed extensively, nor is it necessary to apply all the lesson types presented above, as it would be if the material were presented for the first time. Rather, it should be largely a matter of questioning, discussing, reading the text, and similar activities designed to ascertain what the children have retained of material already covered, to correct any false ideas, to refresh the children on any topics which have become hazy or partly forgotten, and, in general, to recall the main doctrines of the Creed and the basic material concerning the first three commandments. All this is meant to serve as a background against which the study of this year's material in Units Two to Five will be developed.

Let the key idea in this review be to show the greatness and goodness of God and our duty to love Him in return. Let the attitude of the teacher be: Look, see how great God is. How good He has been to us, what love Christ has shown to us, especially in giving us the Church. This year we shall learn how we can and should show our gratitude for these great gifts. By learning how to keep the commandments and by imitating the virtues of Christ, using the means of grace He has given us, we shall best repay, at least in part, our debt to Him.

III. OUTLINE OF SUBJECT MATTER FOR UNIT I (*Review Unit*)

(An experienced teacher or priest may prefer to teach directly from these outlines rather than from the text, using the book for pupil study and drill.)

CHAPTER 1. The Apostles' Creed

I. I Believe in God

  A. God, a Supreme Being
    1. Eternal
    2. All-knowing
    3. All-present
    4. Almighty

  B. The Blessed Trinity
    1. One God
    2. Three Divine Persons: Father, Son, and Holy Ghost

II. I Believe in God the Father, Creator

  A. Angels, created spirits without bodies
    1. Purpose
      a) To praise God
      b) To act as messengers from God
      c) To serve as Guardian Angels
    2. Fall of Bad Angels
      a) Rebelled against God
      b) Followed Lucifer
      c) Were cast into hell

  B. Man, made to the image and likeness of God
    1. Purpose
      a) To know God
      b) To love God
      c) To serve God
      d) To be happy with God in eternity
    2. Fall of Adam and Eve
      a) Disobeyed God
      b) Lost sanctifying grace
      c) Closed gates of heaven
    3. Original Sin
      a) Suffered by all mankind
      b) Did not affect Mary, the Mother of God
    4. Actual Sin
      a) Venial sin
      b) Mortal sin

III. I Believe in God the Son, Redeemer

  A. Jesus Christ, the Son of God became man
    1. To free man from his sins
    2. To reopen the gates of heaven

  B. Jesus Christ, the Second Person of the Blessed Trinity
    1. Divine Nature — God
    2. Human Nature — Man

  C. Jesus Christ, the Son of God
    1. Was born of the Blessed Virgin Mary
    2. On Christmas Day in Bethlehem

D. Jesus Christ, the Redeemer
  1. Suffered under Pontius Pilate
  2. Was crucified, died, and was buried
  3. Descended into hell — a place of rest called Limbo
  4. Rose from the dead glorious and immortal on Easter Sunday
E. Jesus Christ ascended into heaven
  1. Sits at the right hand of God, the Father
  2. Will come to judge the living and the dead

IV. I Believe in God the Holy Ghost, Sanctifier
  A. The Holy Ghost, the third Person of the Blessed Trinity
    1. Sanctifies us through the gift of grace
      a) Sanctifying Grace
      b) Actual Grace
    2. Sanctifies us through the theological virtues
      a) Faith
      b) Hope
      c) Charity
    3. Sanctifies us through the seven gifts
      a) Wisdom
      b) Understanding
      c) Counsel
      d) Fortitude
      e) Knowledge
      f) Piety
      g) Fear of the Lord
  B. Principal ways to obtain grace
    1. Prayer
    2. Sacraments
    3. Sacramentals

V. I Believe in the Holy Catholic Church
  A. The Church a congregation of all baptized persons united in these ways:
    1. Believe the same truths
    2. Offer the same sacrifice
    3. Receive the same sacraments
    4. Governed by the same visible head, the Pope
      (Here review concept of Church as Mystical Body, Gr. 4.)
  B. Jesus Christ, Founder of the Catholic Church
    1. Power given to Peter and Apostles
    2. Power passed on to successors
  C. The True Church
    1. One
    2. Holy
    3. Catholic or Universal
    4. Apostolic

VI. I Believe in the Communion of Saints . . . Forgiveness of Sins
  A. The Union of all who belong to the Church
    1. Church Militant
    2. Church Suffering
    3. Church Triumphant

B. Christ forgave sins
  1. Gave same power to Apostles
  2. Gave same power to successors

VII. I Believe in the Resurrection of the Body and Life Everlasting
  A. Bodies of all people will rise
    1. Souls reunited to their bodies
    2. Will remain so for all eternity
  B. General judgment of living and dead
    1. Reward the good
    2. Punish the evil

CHAPTER 2. The First Three Commandments of God — Love of God

I. God's Law of Love
  A. What it is: Thou shalt love the Lord thy God with thy whole heart, and with thy whole mind, and with thy whole strength.
  B. What it commands:
    1. Love the Lord thy God
    2. With thy whole heart, whole mind, whole strength

II. The First Commandment of God
  A. What it is: I am the Lord thy God; thou shalt not have strange Gods before me.
  B. What it commands:
    1. Supreme worship of God
    2. Acts of faith
    3. Acts of hope
    4. Acts of charity
  C. What it forbids:
    1. Taking part in non-Catholic worship
    2. Presumption
    3. Despair
    4. Hatred of God
    5. Sloth
    6. Envy
    7. Scandal
  D. What it permits and encourages:
    1. Honoring of saints
    2. Petitioning of saints
    3. Honoring of images and statues

III. The Second Commandment of God
  A. What it is: Thou shalt not take the name of the Lord thy God in vain.
  B. What it commands:
    1. To speak with reverence of God
    2. To speak with reverence of the saints
    3. To speak with reverence of all holy things
  C. What it forbids:
    1. Irreverent use of God's name
    2. Cursing
    3. Swearing
    4. All profane language

IV. The Third Commandment
  A. What it is: Remember thou keep holy the Lord's day.

B. What it commands:
1. Worship God in special manner
2. Assist at Holy Mass

C. What it forbids: Unnecessary servile work

IV. ANSWER KEY TO END-UNIT TESTS IN TEXTBOOK

THE CREED (Text, *Living Like Christ in Christ*, pp. 46–48)

TO PROVE MY MASTERY

PART I: Matching — Match the term given in Column I with its meaning in Column II.

Column I	*Column II*
A. Apostles' Creed	1. A less serious offense against the law of God (1) F
B. Mortal sin	2. Three Divine Persons in one God (2) E
C. Angels and men	3. Contains the chief truths taught by the Church (3) A
D. Eternal	4. A grievous offense against the law of God (4) B
E. Blessed Trinity	5. Chief creatures of God (5) C
F. Venial sin	6. Always was and always will be (6) D
G. Theological virtues	7. Judgment immediately after death (7) I
H. One, holy, catholic, apostolic	8. Chief marks of the Church (8) H
I. Particular judgment	9. Faith, hope, and charity (9) G
J. Redemption	10. Offering of Christ's sufferings and death to God in satisfaction for the sins of man (10) J

PART II: Answer these with YES or NO.

1. Does the Holy Ghost sanctify souls through the gift of sanctifying grace? — 1. (Yes)
2. Is hope the virtue by which we firmly believe all the truths revealed by God? — 2. (No)
3. At the end of the world will our Lord come to judge every one who has ever lived on earth? — 3. (Yes)
4. Does sanctifying grace give us a right to heaven? — 4. (Yes)
5. Is the Holy Father the successor of St. Peter? — 5. (Yes)
6. Did Christ make St. John the head of the Apostles? — 6. (No)
7. Is wisdom one of the gifts of the Holy Ghost? — 7. (Yes)
8. Does Christ have two natures? — 8. (Yes)
9. Did Christ rise from the dead on the feast of the Ascension? — 9. (No)
10. Do the good angels help us by praying for us? — 10. (Yes)

PART III: Choose the correct answer.

1. When we say that God can do all things we mean that He is: A. eternal; *B. almighty;* C. all-knowing.
2. The chief truths taught by Jesus Christ through the Catholic Church are found in the: A. Act of Love; B. Our Father; *C. Apostles' Creed.*
3. A grievous offense against the law of God is called: *A. mortal sin;* B. venial sin; C. original sin.
4. The offering of Christ's sufferings and death to God to make up for the sins of men is called the: A. Resurrection; B. Incarnation; *C. Redemption.*
5. The gift of grace is given to us by: *A. God the Holy Ghost;* B. the Pope; C. the Bishop.
6. The union of the faithful on earth, the blessed in heaven, and the souls in purgatory with Christ as their head refers to the: A. forgiveness of sins; *B. communion of saints;* C. resurrection of the body.
7. The judgment which will be passed on each person immediately after death is called the: A. general judgment; B. immediate judgment; *C. particular judgment.*
8. The first bishops of the Church were the: A. fathers of the Church; *B. apostles;* C. disciples.
9. The virtue by which we firmly trust that God will give us eternal happiness and the means to obtain it is: A. faith; *B. hope;* C. charity.
10. Christ rose from the dead on: A. Good Friday; *B. Easter Sunday;* C. Ascension Thursday.

PART IV: Matching beginnings and endings of sentences.

A. *Beginnings:*
1. The words "infinitely perfect" refer to God who is 1. (F)
2. Only God is almighty because 2. (D)
3. Mortal sin is called mortal 3. (G)
4. After Adam and Eve sinned, God 4. (J)
5. By the virtue of Faith 5. (E)
6. Jesus Christ founded the Church to 6. (A)
7. By the virtue of charity we practice 7. (H)
8. The priests, especially parish priests 8. (B)
9. All people are obliged to belong 9. (I)
10. The particular judgment will take place 10. (C)

B. *Endings:*
A. bring all men to salvation.
B. assist the bishops in the care of souls.
C. immediately after death.
D. He alone has the power to do all things.
E. we believe all the truths God has revealed.
F. perfect without limit.
G. because it takes away the life of the soul.
H. love of God, our neighbor, and ourselves.

I. to the Catholic Church in some way, in order to be saved.

J. promised to send a Redeemer to free man from sin and reopen the gates of heaven.

PART V: Complete these sentences by filling in the correct words:

1. When we say that Christt descended into hell, we mean that after He died, the soul of Christ descended into (1).

2. Christ has two natures: the nature of (2) and the nature of (3).*

3. The chief marks of the Church are four: They are (4), (5), (6), and (7).

4. The seven gifts of the Holy Ghost are: (8), (9), (10), (11), (12), (13), and (14).

1. (Limbo)
2. (God)
3. (Man)
4. (one)
5. (holy)
6. (Catholic or universal)
7. (Apostolic)
8. (wisdom)
9. (understanding)
10. (counsel)
11. (fortitude)
12. (knowledge)
13. (piety)
14. (fear of the Lord)

THE FIRST THREE COMMANDMENTS (Text, *Living Like Christ, in Christ*, pp. 58–59)

TO PROVE MY MASTERY

PART I: Matching — Match the term given in Column I with its meaning in Column II.

Column I

A. Cursing
B. Sunday
C. First Commandment
D. Servile work
E. Revealed
F. Sloth
G. Images
H. Presumption
I. Reverence
J. Third Commandment
K. Charity
L. Second Commandment
M. Hope
N. Faith
O. Despair

Column II

1. Remember thou keep holy the Lord's Day. (1) J
2. Calling down evil on a person, place, or thing. (2) A
3. The Lord's Day. (3) B
4. Statues or pictures. (4) G
5. Great respect. (5) I
6. Thinking we can get to heaven without earning it. (6) H
7. I am the Lord thy God; thou shalt not have strange gods before me. (7) C
8. Belief in God and in His truths. (8) N
9. Thou shalt not take the name of the Lord thy God in vain. (9) L
10. Firm trust. (10) M
11. Made known by God to man. (11) E
12. Laziness. (12) F
13. Labor of the body more than of the mind. (13) D
14. Loss of hope in God's mercy. (14) O
15. Love. (15) K

* It is not necessary to follow the *order* of the answers given here. E.g. 2. (Man) and 3. (God) is just as correct as 2. (God) and 3. (Man). This observation applies throughout for these completion exercises.

PART II: Choose the correct answer.

1. The Second Commandment tells us to: A. honor God's name; B. go to Mass on Sunday; C. speak the truth always.

2. We are keeping the Third Commandment if we: A. assist at Mass on Sunday; B. try to obey our parents; C. speak the truth always.

3. When we think that God will take us to heaven even if we do not use the means He has given us to save our souls, we sin against: A. faith; B. hope; C. charity.

4. To curse means to: A. swear; B. wish evil to someone; C. speak an untruth.

5. We practice the virtue of hope when we: A. trust God; B. show respect for priests; C. love our parents.

6. By the First Commandment, we are taught to: A. go to confession often; B. worship God alone; C. respect the property of others.

7. One who gives scandal sins against: A. faith; B. hope; C. charity.

8. Servile work requires: A. labor of body; B. labor of mind; C. use of machinery.

9. Images of Christ and of the saints are used in our churches because they: A. are blessed; B. help us to pray; C. are decorations.

10. When we speak with reverence of the saints we practice the: A. First Commandment; B. Second Commandment; C. Third Commandment.

V. SUGGESTED ACTIVITIES

(It is not intended that all of these activities be carried out during the study of this unit; they are suggestions from which each teacher may select those best suited to her needs or wishes.)

1. Have the class compose original chant tones for the Acts of Faith, Hope, and Love.

2. Have the class compose original chant tones for the Apostles' Creed.

3. Draw symbols of Faith, Hope, and Charity.

4. Provide original illustrations for each of the twelve articles of the Apostles' Creed.

5. Have the children prepare a Vocabulary Chart on which to list new words and terms as they are encountered in the study of the unit.

6. Prepare a class notebook to which children contribute original drawings and compositions based on the study of this unit.

7. Ask the children to keep individual notebooks for original drawings and compositions.

8. Request an original drawing of the tablet of stone upon which God inscribed the first three commandments.

9. Have the children prepare illustrations to show how the first three commandments of God are kept.

10. Propose original problems for discussing ways of observing the first three commandments of God.

VI. BIBLIOGRAPHY

FOR PUPILS:

Bandas, Rev. Rudolph G., and a School Sister of Notre Dame, *The Vine and the Branches;* Highway to Heaven Series, Book V (Milwaukee: Bruce Publishing Company, 1934).

Brennan, Rev. Gerald T., *Angel Food* (Milwaukee: Bruce Publishing Company, 1939).

——— *For Heaven's Sake* (Milwaukee: Bruce Publishing Company, 1942).

——— *Just for Juniors* (Milwaukee: Bruce Publishing Company, 1948).

——— *God Died at Three O'Clock* (Milwaukee: Bruce Publishing Company, 1947).

Diamond, Rev. Wilfrid J., *Heavenwords* (Milwaukee: Bruce Publishing Company, 1947).

Dom Virgil Michel and Dom Basil Stegmann, *A Child of God;* Christ-Life Series in Religion, Book III (New York: The Macmillan Company, 1935).

Dooley, Rev. Lester M., *Hello Halo!* (New York: Wagner, 1947).

Doty, Rev. William L., *Catechetical Stories for Children* (New York: Joseph F. Wagner, Inc., 1948).

E.S., *Poems for God's Children* (Paterson, N. J.: St. Anthony Guild Press, 1946).

Fitzpatrick, Edward A., *The Life of the Soul;* Highway to Heaven Series, Book III (Milwaukee: Bruce Publishing Company, 1933).

——— *The Highway to God;* Highway to Heaven Series, Books VII–VIII (Milwaukee: Bruce Publishing Company, 1933).

Greenstock, David L., *Christopher's Talks to Catholic Children,* Book I (London: Burns, Oates, 1946).

School Sister of Notre Dame, *Before Christ Came;* Highway to Heaven Series, Book IV (Milwaukee: Bruce Publishing Company, 1934).

FOR TEACHERS:

Baierl, Joseph J., *The Creed Explained* (St. Paul: Catechetical Guild, 1945).

Cavanagh, William J., *A Manual for Teachers of Religion* (Milwaukee: Bruce Publishing Company).

Drinkwater, J., *Teaching the Catechism* (Westminster, Md.: The Newman Press, 1952).

Lovasik, Lawrence G., *Catechism in Stories* (Milwaukee: Bruce Publishing Company, 1956).

——— *The Catholic Picture Bible* (New York: Catholic Book Publishing Company).

Tonne, Arthur, *Talks on the Creed* (St. Louis: B. Herder Book Company).

——— *Talks for Children* (St. Louis: B. Herder Book Company).

VII. AUDIO-VISUAL AIDS

Illustrations: "The New Testament"; "The Old Testament" (New York: Catholic Book Publishing Company).

Wall Map: The Life of Christ in the Holy Land Map. Brother Placid, O.S.B. (Collegeville, Minn.: The Liturgical Press).

Filmstrips and accompanying records. "The Life of Jesus," Brother Fidelis Mous (St. Paul: Catechetical Guild).

The St. John's Catechism in Sound Filmstrip, The Creed, St. John's University, Brooklyn, N. Y. (New York: The Declan X. McMullen Company).

Illustrations: The Creed: Maryknoll Sisters, Maryknoll, N. Y.

UNIT II: *THE LAST SEVEN COMMANDMENTS OF GOD, LOVE OF NEIGHBOR*

(Text, *Living Like Christ, in Christ*, pp. 61–111)

I. OBJECTIVES

A. To further our knowledge of the positive and negative aspects of each commandment.

B. To develop an understanding that the commandments are intended to aid us in attaining our eternal salvation.

C. To motivate the observance of the commandments in daily living.

D. To engender a love of the *virtues* which the commandments prescribe, i.e., positive religion, not merely negative.

II. TEACHER PRESENTATION OF UNIT II

The chief goal of the teacher in this Unit is to give the children adequate and accurate knowledge of the moral obligations of a Christian life as defined by the Commandments governing love of self and love of neighbor.

The Commandments are expressed in negative form—"Thou shalt not." Thus it is of highest importance that the teacher should conclude the discussions of the individual commandments by focusing attention upon the Christian virtue which covers the same obligation, but from a positive, not a negative, point of view. For example, in summing up the teaching on the Fourth Commandment attention could be called to the nobility and heroic quality of obedience, stressing the example of Christ and the obedience of His saints, such as St. Paul. At the end of the Fifth Commandment there could be a discussion of the heroism required to practice temperance, the patient, day-by-day control of appetite for food and drink.

Present the Fourth Commandment with this thought in mind: Who was Christ? — God. Yet look how He obeyed. Hence, if I am to be "another Christ," a living member of His Mystical Body, His outward face to the world, my example must be like His. Now is the time to begin my imitation of Christ — in the home and in the classroom.

In presenting the Fifth Commandment help the children see that harm to my own supernatural life or that of my neighbors is far worse than any harm I might do to my own body or that of my neighbors. Hit hard at scandal in all its forms, i.e., leading or influencing others to commit present or future sins by my bad example: swearing, disobeying, wearing immodest clothing, stealing, urging others to do wrong.

In presenting the Sixth and Ninth Commandments stress modesty as the best safeguard of purity. Encourage modesty of the eyes. Urge the girls especially to respect modesty and to respect others by never becoming occasions of sin through immodest dress. Warn them of the temptations they cause boys and men by their vanity, their lack of courage in avoiding immodest clothing or behavior. Warn them of their grave obligations in this matter. Remind them of the heroism of St. Maria Goretti who saved her own soul and also helped the man who wanted her to commit sin do penance for his evil deeds. Perhaps the source of his trouble was immodestly clothed women who had aroused his emotions.

In handling the Seventh and Tenth Commandments stress the detachment of the Holy Family from desires for great worldly goods. Praise those who, having the world's goods, live simply, unostentatiously, helping those who have little. "If thou wilt be perfect . . . go, sell what thou hast." Discuss modern advertising and the temptations it brings many families, causing them to go into debt just to add to their material goods. Discuss the problems of restitution and of poverty in other nations.

In presenting the Eighth Commandment pay special attention to sins against charity, especially those caused by talking about our neighbors, envying them for their goods, etc. Emphasize the practice of pointing out some good trait or deed of a person who is being calumniated.

III. OUTLINE OF SUBJECT MATTER FOR UNIT II

CHAPTER 3. Honor Thy Father and Thy Mother

I. The Fourth Commandment
  A. What it is: Honor thy father and thy mother.
    1. Authority from God
    2. Delegated to parents
    3. Delegated to lawful superiors
  B. What it commands:
    1. Respect, love, and obedience to parents
    2. Respect, love, and obedience to all lawful superiors

C. What it forbids:
1. Disrespect, unkindness, and disobedience to parents
2. Disrespect, unkindness, and disobedience to all lawful superiors

CHAPTER 4. Thou Shalt Not Kill

I. The Fifth Commandment
A. What it is: Thou shalt not kill.
1. Supernatural life (Spiritual life)
2. Natural life (Bodily life)
B. What it commands:
1. Proper care of our own spiritual life
2. Proper care of our bodily life
3. Proper care of spiritual life of our neighbor
4. Proper care of bodily life of our neighbor
C. What it forbids:
1. Suicide
2. Murder
3. Anger
4. Hatred
5. Revenge
6. Fighting
7. Drunkenness
8. Bad example

CHAPTER 5. Thou Shalt Not Commit Adultery

I. The Sixth Commandment
A. What it is: Thou shalt not commit adultery. It is often called the commandment of purity.
B. What it commands:
1. Purity in outward behavior
2. Modesty in outward behavior
C. Supernatural aids to purity
1. Holy Mass
2. Prayer
3. Sacraments
D. Natural aids to purity
1. Approved recreations
2. Worthwhile hobbies
E. What it forbids:
1. Impurity in words, looks, and actions
2. Immodesty in words, looks, and actions

CHAPTER 6. Thou Shalt Not Steal

I. The Seventh Commandment
A. What it is: Thou shalt not steal.
1. Called the commandment of justice
2. Refers to the use of worldly goods
B. What it commands:
1. To know that all have a right to property
2. To respect the property of others
3. To restore stolen goods or their value.

C. What it forbids:
1. Dishonesty
2. Stealing
3. Cheating
4. Unjust keeping of property of others
5. Unjust damage to property of others

CHAPTER 7. Thou Shalt Not Bear False Witness Against Thy Neighbor

I. The Eighth Commandment
A. What it is: Thou shalt not bear false witness against thy neighbor.
1. Power of speech, a gift from God
2. Power of speech, to be used for God's honor
B. What it commands:
1. To speak the truth in all things
2. To respect the good name of our neighbor
C. What it forbids:
1. To speak an untruth
2. To harm the good name of our neighbor
3. To form rash judgment concerning our neighbor

CHAPTER 8. Thou Shalt Not Covet Thy Neighbor's Wife

I. The ninth commandment
A. What it is: Thou shalt not covet thy neighbor's wife.
B. What it commands:
1. To be pure in thought
2. To be pure in desire
C. Supernatural aids to purity:
1. Holy Mass
2. Prayer
3. Sacraments
D. Natural aids to purity:
1. Approved recreations
2. Worthwhile hobbies
E. What it forbids:
1. Willful impure thoughts
2. Willful impure desires

CHAPTER 9. Thou Shalt Not Covet Thy Neighbor's Goods

I. The tenth commandment
A. What it is: Thou shalt not covet thy neighbor's goods.
1. Commandment of justice
2. Regulates our desires for material goods.
B. What it commands:
To be satisfied with what we have
C. What it forbids:
1. To desire to take or keep unjustly what belongs to another
2. To be envious of the success of another

IV. ANSWER KEY TO END-UNIT TESTS IN TEXTBOOK

THE LAST SEVEN COMMANDMENTS OF GOD (Text, *Living Like Christ, in Christ,* pp. 110–111)

TO PROVE MY MASTERY

PART I: Which commandments tell us to do the following?

1. To love and obey our parents.   1. 4
2. To be truthful at all times.   2. 8
3. To eat proper food and get enough rest.   3. 5
4. To return any article we have borrowed.   4. 7
5. To watch only approved movies and television programs.   5. 5–6
6. To respect and obey our teachers.   6. 4
7. To give good example to our neighbor.   7. 5
8. To be pure in word and act.   8. 6
9. To try not to fight with companions.   9. 5
10. To be satisfied with the amount of spending money our parents give us.   10. 10
11. To pray to the Blessed Virgin when tempted against purity.   11. 6–9
12. To try to locate the owner of any article we may find.   12. 7
13. To avoid unkind talk about our neighbor.   13. 8
14. To keep away from companions who lead us into sin.   14. 5
15. To pay for any damage done to the property of others.   15. 7

PART II: Complete these sentences by filling in the correct words:

1. My body is the temple of the (1).   1. (Holy Ghost)
2. The sixth commandment requires me to be pure in (2), (3), and (4).   2. (word)
3. The fourth commandment tells us that we must (5) and (6) our parents.   3. (looks)
4. We must live our lives according to (7) plan.   4. (actions)
5. We must take care of our own and of our neighbor's (8) and (9) well-being.   5. (respect)
6. The seventh commandment forbids all (10).   6. (love)
7. A great help in keeping the tenth commandment is to be (11) with what we have.   7. (God's)
8. The ninth commandment refers to our (12) and (13).   8. (spiritual)
9. We must (14) any damage we have unjustly caused.   9. (bodily)
10. We sin against the eighth commandment by telling (15).   10. (dishonesty)

11. (satisfied)
12. (thoughts)
13. (desires)
14. (repair)
15. (lies)

PART III: Choose the correct answer:

1. I must love and obey my parents chiefly because: A. they will punish me;   B. they love me and take care of me;   *C. they take the place of God.*
2. When parents become old they should be taken care of: *A. by their children;*   B. by the Catholic Charities;   C. by the city.
3. The fifth commandment forbids: A. missing Mass on Sundays;   B. telling lies;   *C. murder, suicide, fighting, and bad example.*
4. Some means of helping us to be pure are: A. reading all kinds of comic books;   *B. going to confession and Holy Communion often;*   C. attending any kind of movie.
5. If we have stolen or unjustly damaged another's property we are obliged to: A. tell our parents;   *B. restore the goods or their value;*   C. pay for only a part of the damage.
6. If someone is telling an unkind story about another person we should: *A. try to say something good about that person;*   B. listen attentively to the story;   C. repeat the story to others.
7. The ninth commandment tells us: A. to be just;   *B. to be pure in thought and desire;*   C. to speak truthfully.

V. SUGGESTED ACTIVITIES

1. Compositions explaining each of the last seven commandments.
2. Cartoon drawings showing how we practice the last seven commandments.
3. Original symbols for each of the commandments, four to ten.
4. Dramatizations showing how we keep the commandments four to ten.
5. Cartoon drawings illustrating the spiritual and corporal works of mercy.
6. Original problems for discussing the way we keep the commandments four to ten.
7. A vocabulary chart on which children list new words and terms encountered during the study of this unit.
8. Class or individual notebooks for original drawings and compositions based on the study of this unit.
9. A diagram showing how God delegates authority to our various lawful superiors.
10. Have the children read about St. Thomas Aquinas, St. Maria Goretti, or some other saints who can be called models of purity.
11. Have children find out, report on, and discuss living conditions, wages, poverty in other nations and our obligation to help them rise from grinding poverty and degradation.

VI. BIBLIOGRAPHY

FOR PUPILS:

Bandas, Rev. Rudolph G., and a School Sister of Notre Dame, *The Vine and the Branches;* Highway to Heaven Series, Book V (Milwaukee: Bruce Publishing Company, 1934).

Brennan, Rev. Gerald T., *Going His Way* (Milwaukee: Bruce Publishing Company, 1945).

——— *Just for Juniors* (Milwaukee: Bruce Publishing Company, 1948).

Dom Virgil Michel and Dom Basil Stegmann, *A Child of God;* Christ-Life Series in Religion, Book IV (New York: The Macmillan Company, 1935).

Doty, Rev. William L., *Catechetical Stories for Children* (New York: Joseph F. Wagner, Inc., 1948).

Fitzpatrick, Edward A., *The Highway to God;* Highway to Heaven Series, Books VII–VIII (Milwaukee: Bruce Publishing Company, 1933).

Gasparri, Peter Cardinal, *Catholic Faith, Book II* (New York: P. J. Kenedy and Sons, 1939).

Kelly, Rev. William R., and Sister Mary Imelda, and Rev. M. A. Schumacher, *Living for God;* Living My Religion Series, Book IV (New York: Benziger Brothers, Inc., 1947).

——— *Living Through God's Gifts;* Living My Religion Series, Book V (New York: Benziger Brothers, Inc., 1947).

Roche, Rev. Thomas B., *The Commandments of God* (Boston: Mission Church Press, 1940).

FOR TEACHERS:

Baierl, Joseph J., *The Commandments Explained* (St. Paul: Catechetical Guild, 1945).

Doty, William L., *Catechetical Stories for Children* (New York: Joseph F. Wagner, Inc., 1948).

Greenstock, David L., *Christopher's Talks to Children, Vol. II* (London: Burns, Oates, 1946).

Hosty, Thomas, *Good Morning, Boys and Girls* (New York: Catholic Book Publishing Company).

Schumacher, Rev. M. A., *How to Teach the Catechism, Vol. II* (New York: Benziger Brothers, Inc., 1934).

——— *I Teach Catechism*, Vols. II and III (New York: Benziger Brothers, Inc., 1946).

Tonne, Rev. Arthur, *Prayer, Precepts, and Virtues* (St. Louis: B. Herder Book Company).

——— *Talks on the Commandments* (St. Louis: B. Herder Book Company).

VII. AUDIO-VISUAL AIDS

Illustrations: The Commandments (St. Paul: Catechetical Guild).

Illustrations: I Learn God's Laws. Maryknoll Sisters, Maryknoll, N. Y.

Sound Filmstrip: The Ten Commandments (St. Paul: Catechetical Guild).

The St. John's Catechism in Sound Filmstrip: The Commandments in General; The First Commandment of God. St. John's University, Brooklyn, N. Y. (New York: The Declan X. McMullen Company).

UNIT III: THE COMMANDMENTS OF THE CHURCH

(Text, *Living Like Christ, in Christ*, pp. 112–144)

I. OBJECTIVES

A. To develop the understanding that the laws of the Church help us reach our eternal goal.

B. To increase the knowledge of what the laws of the Church command and what they forbid.

C. To stress the fact that the authority of the Church, like all authority, comes from God.

D. To encourage deeper appreciation of the Church as a Mother.

II. TEACHER PRESENTATION OF UNIT III

God allows His Church to make laws to help us reach heaven. The Church has many laws, and of these we shall study the six principal ones which have bearing for the laity.

Teach the children that the habit of observing these laws from youth will make it much easier for them to keep these laws in later life. Warn them to have courage in the face of bad example. Challenge them to show they are not weaklings but have real Christian backbone that will make them proud to say they are Catholics. Let them know that it takes real courage and consistent practice to build good habits.

Encourage weekly confession and weekly or more frequent Communion as an ideal, but do not set such high ideals that scruples might result. Perhaps you might suggest bimonthly or monthly confession as a reasonable criterion, with weekly confession as a highly desirable demand. Encourage the children to develop dependence on themselves in these matters. Wean them from the childhood habit of going to the sacraments only when led and encourage them to develop the habits needed for adult life — going to Confession and Communion of their own will and desire.

III. OUTLINE OF SUBJECT MATTER FOR UNIT III

CHAPTER 10. The Six Chief Commandments of the Church

I. Authority of the Church

A. Source of authority: God
1. Delegated from Christ to Peter
2. Passed from Peter to successors

B. Purpose for this authority
1. Right to make laws
2. Right to change laws
3. Right to enforce laws
4. Right to punish those who disobey laws

II. Six chief laws of the Church

A. What they are
1. To assist at Mass on all Sundays and holydays of obligation.
2. To fast and abstain on the days appointed.
3. To confess our sins at least once a year.
4. To receive Holy Communion during the Easter time.
5. To contribute to the support of the Church.
6. To observe the laws of the Church concerning marriage.

B. Purpose of these laws
1. To help us keep the commandments of God.
2. To help us live our lives according to the teaching of Christ.

CHAPTER 11. Assist at Mass on Sundays and Holydays of Obligation

I. The first Law of the Church

A. What it is: To assist at Mass on Sundays and holydays of obligation
1. Concerns Mass on Sundays
2. Concerns Mass on holydays of obligation

B. What it commands:
1. To assist at Mass on all Sundays
2. To assist at Mass on holydays of obligation
   a) Christmas
   b) Octave of the Nativity of Our Lord
   c) Ascension Thursday
   d) Assumption
   e) All Saints' Day
   f) Immaculate Conception

C. What it forbids:
1. To miss Mass without sufficient reason
2. To be late for Mass without sufficient reason
3. To do servile work unnecessarily

CHAPTER 12. Fast and Abstain on the Days Appointed

I. The second law of the Church
  A. What it is: To fast and abstain on the days appointed
    1. Acts of self-denial
    2. Acts of penance
  B. What it commands
    1. To fast on days appointed
      a) Only one full meal allowed
      b) Applies to persons between ages of twenty-one and fifty-nine
      c) The appointed days are:
        1. Weekdays of Lent
        2. Ember days
        3. Vigil of Pentecost
        4. Day before the feast of the Immaculate Conception
        5. Day before All Saints' Day (some bishops regularly dispense)
        6. December 23 or the Vigil of Christmas
    2. To abstain on days appointed
      a) To keep from eating meat
      b) Applies to every baptized person, seven years of age or over
      c) The days of complete abstinence (no meat allowed):
        1. All Fridays
        2. Ash Wednesday
        3. Day before the feast of the Immaculate Conception
        4. December 23 or the Vigil of Christmas
        5. Holy Saturday (In some dioceses this is a day of fast and partial abstinence.)
      d) The days of partial abstinence (meat may be eaten once at the principal meal):
        1. Wednesdays and Saturdays of Ember Weeks
        2. Vigil of Pentecost
        3. Day before All Saints' Day (some bishops regularly dispense)
  C. What it forbids:
    1. Eating more than is prescribed on appointed days
    2. Eating meat on days prescribed

CHAPTER 13. Confess Our Sins and Receive Holy Communion

I. The third and fourth laws of the Church
  A. What they are: To confess our sins at least once a year; To receive Holy Eucharist during the Easter time
    1. Means of God's grace
    2. Helps to attain heaven
  B. What they command:
    1. To confess our sins any time during the year (at least once)
    2. To receive Holy Communion during the Easter time
    3. Easter time begins first Sunday of Lent and ends on Trinity Sunday
  C. What they forbid:
    1. To neglect the sacrament of Penance for more than a year
    2. To neglect Holy Communion during the Easter time

CHAPTER 14. Contribute to the Support of the Church

I. The fifth law of the Church
  A. What it is: To contribute to the support of the Church
    1. Contribution represents the gift offered in early Church
    2. Used to pay expenses of Church
  B. What it commands:
    1. Each must help pay expenses of parish
    2. Catholics must help support Catholic education and charities
    3. Those who can must help missions
  C. What it forbids:
    1. Failure to recognize responsibilities to parish
    2. Neglect of Catholic schools and charities
    3. Neglect of missions

CHAPTER 15. Observe the Laws of Marriage

I. The sixth law of the Church
  A. What it is: To observe the laws of the Church concerning marriage
    1. God loved marriage
    2. Christ made marriage a sacrament
  B. What it commands:
    1. To marry a Catholic
    2. To be married in the presence of an authorized priest
    3. To be married in the presence of two witnesses
    4. Witnesses must be good, practicing Catholics
    5. Should be married in parish church at a Nuptial Mass
  C. What it forbids:
    1. To marry a non-Catholic without special dispensation
    2. To marry during Lent or Advent without special permission
    3. Marriage in the presence of Protestant ministers or Justice of Peace

IV. ANSWER KEY TO END-UNIT TESTS IN TEXTBOOK

THE COMMANDMENTS OF THE CHURCH (Text, *Living Like Christ, in Christ*, p. 144)

TO PROVE MY MASTERY

PART I: Complete the following sentences:

The chief laws of the Church are:

1. To assist at Mass: (on Sundays and holydays of obligation).
2. To fast and abstain on: (the days appointed).
3. To confess our sins: (at least once a year).
4. To receive Holy Communion: (during the Easter time).
5. To contribute to the: (support of the Church).
6. To observe the laws of the Church: (concerning marriage).

PART II: Which Commandment of the Church is kept in each of these cases?

1. Catholics are married at a Nuptial Mass.   1. 6
2. We help around the church or school property without pay.   2. 5
3. We don't eat meat on Friday.   3. 2
4. We attend Mass on Sundays.   4. 1
5. We give money to the Church.   5. 5
6. Grown people eat only one full meal on days appointed by the Church.   6. 2
7. We assist at Mass on All Saints' Day.   7. 1
8. We receive Holy Communion during the Easter time.   8. 4
9. Persons in mortal sin make a good confession once a year. 9. 3
10. We give money to the missions.   10. 5

PART III: Matching — Match the term given in Column I with its meaning in Column II.

Column I	Column II
A. November 1	1. Age for fasting. (1) F
B. Assumption	2. No meat may be eaten. (2) H
C. Ascension Day	3. A day on which we must assist at Mass. (3) J
D. Easter Time	4. Forty days after Easter. (4) C
E. Vigil	5. To eat only one full meal. (5) G
F. 21–59	6. Feast of All Saints. (6) A
G. Fast Day	7. Mary was taken up into heaven. (7) B
H. Complete Abstinence	8. The day before a feast. (8) E
I. Partial Abstinence	9. First Sunday of Lent to Trinity Sunday. (9) D
J. Holyday	

V. SUGGESTED ACTIVITIES

1. Draw a dome representing St. Peter's Church. Show the power extending from St. Peter's to bishop over diocese, pastor over individual parish.

2. Plan reports in which the six holydays of obligation are explained.
3. Learn the Grace Before and After Meals.
4. Make a time line for the Easter time.
5. Plan original prayers: prayers of thanksgiving for the sacraments of Penance and Holy Eucharist, prayers of spiritual communion.
6. Diagram the various ways in which we can support the Church.
7. Plan reports on mission activities both foreign and home.
8. Make a vocabulary chart on which new words and terms learned in this unit will be printed.
9. Plan original skits showing how the laws of the Church are practiced.

VI. BIBLIOGRAPHY

FOR PUPILS:

Bandas, Rev. Rudolph G., and a School Sister of Notre Dame, *The Vine and the Branches*; Highway to Heaven Series, Book V (Milwaukee: Bruce Publishing Company, 1934).

Doty, Rev. William L., *Catechetical Stories for Children* (New York: Joseph F. Wagner, Inc., 1948).

Fitzpatrick, Edward A., *The Life of the Soul*; Highway to Heaven Series, Book III (Milwaukee: Bruce Publishing Company, 1933).

———— *The Highway to God*; Highway to Heaven Series, Books VII–VIII (Milwaukee: Bruce Publishing Company, 1933).

Gasparri, Peter Cardinal, *Catholic Faith, Book II* (New York: P. J. Kenedy and Sons, 1939).

———— *Catholic Faith, Book III* (New York: P. J. Kenedy and Sons, 1938).

Kelly, Rev. William R. and Sister Mary Imelda and Rev. M. A. Schumacher, *Living for God*; Living My Religion Series, Book IV (New York: Benziger Brothers, Inc., 1947).

———— *Living in God's Church*; Living My Religion Series, Book VI (New York: Benziger Brothers, Inc., 1948).

Mother Bolton, Religious of the Cenacle, *The Spiritual Way*; Book IV (New York: World Book Company, 1930).

School Sister of Notre Dame, *Before Christ Came*; Highway to Heaven Series, Book IV (Milwaukee: Bruce Publishing Company, 1934).

FOR TEACHERS:

Aylward, Stephen, *Catechism Comes to Life* (St. Paul: Catechetical Guild Press, 1942).

Baierl, Joseph J., *The Commandments Explained* (St. Paul: Catechetical Guild, 1943).

Bandas, Rudolph, G., *Catechetical Methods* (New York: Joseph F. Wagner, Inc., 1929).

Cavanagh, Rev. William J., *A Manual for Teachers of Religion* (Milwaukee: Bruce Publishing Company).

Doty, William L., *Catechetical Stories for Children* (New York: Joseph F. Wagner, Inc., 1948).

Greenstock, David L., *Christopher's Talks to Children*, Vol. II (London: Burns, Oates, 1946).

Lahey, Rev. Thomas A., *The Children's Friend, A Life of Christ for Children* (St. Louis: B. Herder Book Company).

Lovasik, Rev. Lawrence G., *The Catholic Picture Bible* (New York: Catholic Book Publishing Company).

Schumacher, Rev. M. A., *I Teach Catechism*, Vols. II and III (New York: Benziger Brothers, Inc., 1946).

Tonne, Rev. Arthur, *Prayer, Precepts, and Virtues* (St. Louis: B. Herder Book Company).

———— *Talks on the Commandments* (St. Louis: B. Herder Book Company).

VII. AUDIO-VISUAL AIDS

Illustrations: Symbols for Feasts and Commons, Clemens Schmidt (Collegeville, Minn.: The Liturgical Press).

Illustrations: Commandments of the Church; Liturgical Symbols (St. Paul: Catechetical Guild).

Illustrations: Dramatic Scenes from the Old and New Testament (St. Paul: Catechetical Guild).

UNIT IV: *THE SEVEN SACRAMENTS*

(Text, *Living Like Christ, in Christ*, pp. 145–252)

I. OBJECTIVES

A. To develop an appreciation of the sacraments as a source of grace.

B. To further the understanding of the value of each of the sacraments to our supernatural life.

C. To encourage frequent reception of the sacraments.

D. To incite greater love for the Mass, another source of grace.

E. To increase knowledge of the Mass, the Perfect Unbloody Sacrifice.

II. TEACHER PRESENTATION OF UNIT IV

In the previous year, when the Mystical Body and the liturgy were the central themes of study, the sacraments were presented as the great means of uniting us to Christ and Christ to us. With that knowledge as a point of departure we will study each sacrament in detail in this unit, learning those basic facts which every Catholic has a duty to learn.

As this is the first systematic study by the children of the entire sacramental system and as the material contained in the Number One Catechism is relatively brief, at least in relation to the Number Two Catechism, the teacher should strive to guarantee that all children know the fundamental facts and principles concerning the sacraments, especially those which are most necessary to leading a Christian life and which will assist the students to attain the goal God has made possible for men to win with His help. Do not, however, crowd in too much material from the Number Two Catechism.

III. OUTLINE OF SUBJECT MATTER FOR UNIT IV

CHAPTER 16. The Seven Sacraments: A Means of Grace

I. The sacraments a means of grace
   A. What a sacrament is:
      1. An outward sign
      2. Instituted by Christ
      3. To give grace
   B. The seven sacraments:
      1. Baptism
      2. Confirmation
      3. Holy Eucharist
      4. Penance
      5. Extreme Unction
      6. Matrimony
      7. Holy Orders
   C. Effects of the sacraments:
      1. Give sanctifying grace
      2. Increase sanctifying grace
      3. Give sacramental grace

II. Kinds of sacraments
   A. Sacraments of the Dead
      1. What they do: Give life of grace to souls dead through sin
      2. Which they are:
         a) Baptism
         b) Penance
   B. Sacraments of the Living
      1. What they do: Give more grace to souls already alive through grace
      2. Which they are:
         a) Confirmation
         b) Holy Eucharist
         c) Extreme Unction
         d) Matrimony
         e) Holy Orders

III. Reception of sacraments
   A. Those which imprint a lasting spiritual mark and can be received only once
      1. Baptism
      2. Confirmation
      3. Holy Orders
   B. Those which can be received more than once
      1. Penance
      2. Holy Eucharist
      3. Extreme Unction
      4. Matrimony

CHAPTER 17. Baptism: A New Life of Grace

I. The Sacrament of Baptism
   A. What it is:
      Sacrament of new life
   B. What it does for us:
      1. Gives sanctifying grace
      2. Makes us children of God
      3. Takes away original sin
      4. Takes away actual sins if any are present

C. Who may baptize:
   1. Priest, usual minister
   2. Anyone in an emergency
D. How Baptism is given:
   1. By the priest:
      a) Special baptismal water
      b) Ceremony according to liturgy
   2. By lay person:
      a) Ordinary water
      b) Say while pouring water: "I baptize thee in the name of the Father, and of the Son, and of the Holy Ghost."

CHAPTER 18. Confirmation: Soldiers of Christ

I. The Sacrament of Confirmation
   A. What it is:
      1. Holy Ghost comes in special way
      2. To enable us to profess our faith
   B. What it does for us:
      1. Increases sanctifying grace
      2. Strengthens theological virtues
      3. Strengthens seven gifts
      4. Makes us brave and courageous
      5. Imprints a lasting mark
   C. Who may confirm:
      1. Bishop, usual minister
      2. Priest in case of necessity
   D. How Confirmation is given:
      1. Bishop extends hands over those to be confirmed
      2. Prays that they may receive the Holy Ghost
      3. Anoints the forehead of each with holy chrism in the form of a cross
      4. Speaks the proper words
      5. Gives a slight tap on cheek

CHAPTER 19. The Holy Eucharist: Bread of Life

I. The Sacrament of Holy Eucharist
   A. What it is:
      1. A sacrament } under appearances of bread
      2. A sacrifice } and wine Lord Christ is contained, offered, received
   B. When instituted:
      1. Holy Thursday
      2. Last Supper
   C. How continued:
      1. Power given to apostles
      2. Power given to successors

CHAPTER 20. Holy Mass: The Perfect Sacrifice

I. Meaning of Sacrifice
   A. Act of Worship:
      1. To show love for God
      2. To show recognition of God as creator of heaven and earth and all things
   B. Essentials of sacrifice:
      1. Victim to be offered to God
      2. Priest to offer sacrifice
      3. Altar upon which to offer victim

II. Two Types of Sacrifice
   A. Perfect Bloody Sacrifice
      1. Christ, perfect priest
      2. Christ, perfect victim
      3. Satisfied Almighty God
      4. Reopened gates of heaven
   B. Perfect Unbloody Sacrifice:
      1. Christ, priest and victim
      2. Offered under appearances of bread and wine
      3. The Mass, a re-enactment of perfect bloody sacrifice

III. The Mass, Perfect Unbloody Sacrifice
   A. A sacrifice:
      1. Act of worship
      2. Act of recognition of God as creator
   B. We pray — we speak to God:
      1. Sign of the Cross
      2. Confiteor
      3. Introit
      4. Kyrie
      5. Gloria
      6. Dominus Vobiscum
      7. Collect
   C. We learn — God speaks to us:
      1. Epistle
      2. Gospel
      3. Sermon
   D. Credo
      Nicene Creed
   E. We offer — The first principal part of the Mass:
      1. Offering of large host
      2. Offering of water and wine
      3. Washing of hands
      4. Secret prayers
   F. We sacrifice:
      1. Preface
      2. Remembrance Prayers
         a) Church Militant
         b) Church Triumphant
      3. Consecration — The second principal part of the Mass
      4. Remembrance Prayers
         a) Church Suffering
         b) Church Militant
         c) Through Christ we receive all good things
      5. Minor elevation
   G. We receive and pray
      1. Our Father
      2. "Lamb of God . . . grant us peace."
      3. Priest's Communion — Third principal part of Mass
      4. "Lord, I am not worthy . . . soul shall be healed."
      5. Holy Communion of faithful
      6. Thanksgiving
         a) Communion Prayer
         b) Postcommunion Prayers

7. "Ite Missa est"
8. Last Blessing
9. Last Gospel
10. "Deo gratias"
11. Prayers after Mass

CHAPTER 21. Penance: Love and Mercy

I. The Sacrament of Penance
   A. What it is:
      1. Sacrament of mercy
      2. Sacrament through which actual sins are forgiven
   B. What it does for us:
      1. Takes away actual sin
      2. Restores sanctifying grace
      3. Increases sanctifying grace
   C. How we receive it:
      1. Examination of conscience:
         a) Pray to the Holy Ghost
         b) Call to mind offenses against the Commandments of God and of the Church
      2. Be sorry for our sins:
         a) Perfect contrition: sorrow for sin because we have offended God whom we love
         b) Imperfect contrition: sorrow for sin because we fear God's punishment
      3. Make up our minds not to sin again: Firm resolution not to sin again
      4. Confess our sins to the priest:
         a) Mortal sins must be confessed
         b) Venial sins may be confessed
      5. Be willing to do the penance the priest gives:
         a) Thank God for the sacrament
         b) Say the penance

CHAPTER 22. Temporal Punishment and Indulgences

I. Punishment due to sin.
   A. Eternal punishment:
      1. Eternal — lasting forever
      2. Taken away by a good confession
   B. Temporal punishment:
      1. Temporal — lasting for a time
      2. Sometimes remains to be taken care of by penances during life or in purgatory
II. Indulgences
   A. What they do:
      1. Take away temporal punishment
      2. Draw on the merits of spiritual treasury
      3. May be applied to souls in purgatory
   B. Kinds:
      1. Plenary Indulgence
         a) Remission of all temporal punishment
         b) Means full or complete
      2. Partial Indulgence
         a) Means part or portion of
         b) Remission of only part of temporal punishment

III. How we obtain indulgences:
   A. Be in the state of grace
      1. Free from mortal sin
      2. Soul in sanctifying grace
   B. Desire to gain the indulgence:
      1. Make the intention in Morning Offering
      2. Renew the intention in the course of the day
   C. Perform the works required:
      1. Some require a visit to a church
      2. Some require a recitation of certain prayers
      3. Some require reception of the Sacraments

CHAPTER 23. Extreme Unction: Last Anointing

I. Sacrament of Extreme Unction
   A. What it is:
      1. Sacrament of the Living
      2. Last anointing
      3. Administered at time of danger of death
   B. Effects:
      1. Takes away venial sin
      2. Remits temporal punishment
      3. Strengthens the soul
      4. Sometimes restores strength to the body
      5. Removes the fear of death
      6. Strengthens the gift of fortitude
   C. Personal preparation:
      1. Be in the state of grace
      2. Go to confession if possible
      3. Receive Holy Communion if possible
   D. Material preparation:
      1. Call priest as soon as person becomes seriously sick
      2. Have room neat and clean
      3. Prepare table
         a) cover with white cloth
         b) crucifix
         c) two blessed candles (lighted)
         d) holy water
         e) glass of water and spoon
         f) white napkin or small towel
         g) plate with cotton or bread
      4. Meet the priest at the door with lighted candle if he has the Blessed Sacrament
   E. Administration:
      1. Priest anoints the five senses
      2. Prays that God forgive sins committed by the senses

CHAPTER 24. Holy Orders: "Other Christs"

I. The sacrament of Holy Orders
   A. What it is:
      1. A sacrament of the living
      2. Makes men other Christs
   B. Preparation:
      1. Pray for grace to know God's will
      2. Have the desire to perform the duties of a priest

3. Have good health
4. Be of good character
5. Have more than average intelligence
6. Complete the studies required in the seminary

C. Reception of Holy Orders:
1. Minor Orders
2. Major Orders
3. Ordination by bishop of diocese
   a) Lays hands on deacon
   b) Prays that the Holy Ghost comes to him
   c) Anoints his hands
   d) Presents the sacred vessels

D. Effects:
1. Imprints a lasting mark
2. Increases sanctifying grace
3. Gives power to offer Mass
4. Gives power to administer sacraments
5. Gives power to teach and govern in matters of Church

E. Our appreciation of Holy Orders:
1. Sincere reverence for priests
2. Pray for priests and religious
3. Pray for religious vocations

CHAPTER 25. Matrimony: Lawful Marriage

I. The Sacrament of Matrimony
A. What it is:
1. Sacrament of living
2. Binds man and woman in lawful marriage

B. Lawful Christian Marriage:
1. Bride and groom administer the sacrament
2. Priest witnesses marriage vows
3. Two practicing Catholics as witnesses
4. Nuptial Mass and Communion

C. Holy Family, model of Catholic home:
1. Duties of father:
   a) Head of family
   b) Must support wife and children
   c) Give good example to children
2. Duties of mother:
   a) Must care for home
   b) Take care of needs of husband and children
   c) Give good example to children
3. Duties of children:
   a) Love parents
   b) Obey parents
   c) Respect parents

IV. ANSWER KEY TO END-UNIT TESTS IN TEXTBOOK

A. THE SACRAMENTS — Baptism, Confirmation, Holy Eucharist (Text, *Living Like Christ, in Christ*, pp. 170–172)

TO PROVE MY MASTERY

PART I: Match the beginnings and endings of the following sentences:

Beginnings
1. The sacraments give   (1) C
2. Each sacrament gives a special grace   (2) H
3. The sacrament is an outward sign   (3) A
4. The sacraments have the power of giving grace   (4) F
5. Baptism makes us   (5) E
6. If there is danger that a baby will die without Baptism   (6) G
7. Baptism makes it possible   (7) B
8. Baptism and Penance are called   (8) D

Endings
A. instituted by Christ to give grace.
B. to receive the other sacraments.
C. sanctifying grace if we receive them properly.
D. sacraments of the dead.
E. members of the Church and children of God.
F. because of the merits of Christ.
G. anyone may and should baptize him.
H. called sacramental grace.

PART II: Fill in the missing word or words.

1. Sacraments that can be received more than once are: (1), (2), (3), and (4).
2. One who receives the sacraments of the living in mortal sin commits a: (5).
3. The sacraments of (6), (7), and (8) can be received only once.
4. The sin which we inherit from Adam is (9) sin.
5. The usual minister of Baptism is (10).
6. The sacraments of the (11) give supernatural life of grace to souls spiritually dead through sin.
7. The name of a (12) is given at Baptism so that we may imitate his life and have him for a protector.
8. The most necessary sacrament is (13).
9. (14) grace gives us supernatural life.
10. If I were called upon in an emergency to baptize a dying child, I would do the following (15).
11. Mary's little brother Daniel was baptized last week. List the changes

1. (Holy Eucharist)
2. (Penance)
3. (Extreme Unction)
4. (Matrimony)
5. (sacrilege)
6. (Baptism)
7. (Confirmation)
8. (Holy Orders)
9. (original)
10. (the priest)
11. (dead)
12. (saint)
13. (Baptism)
14. (Sanctifying)
15. (Pour water over the forehead while saying at the same time: "I baptize thee in the name of the Father and of the Son and of the Holy Spirit.")

that took place in Daniel when he was baptized (16).

12. Write the words of Christ to Nicodemus that show that baptism is necessary (17).

16. (Cleansed of original sin, given sanctifying grace, made a child of God and a member of His Church.)

17. ("Unless a man be born again of water and the Holy Spirit he can not enter into the kingdom of God.")

PART III: Answer with YES or NO.

1. Is Confirmation a sacrament of the dead — 1. No
2. Does the sacrament of Confirmation make us soldiers of Jesus Christ? — 2. Yes
3. May we receive the sacrament of Confirmation more than once? — 3. No
4. Is the bishop the usual minister of Confirmation? — 4. Yes
5. Does the Holy Ghost come to us in a special way through Confirmation? — 5. Yes
6. Does Confirmation strengthen us against dangers to salvation? — 6. Yes
7. Should all Catholics be confirmed? — 7. Yes
8. Does Confirmation prepare us to defend our faith? — 8. Yes
9. May a priest ever give the sacrament of Confirmation? — 9. Yes
10. Does the Holy Ghost give us the theological virtues in Confirmation? — 10. No

PART IV: Complete the following sentences:

1. Confirmation is the sacrament through which the Holy Ghost comes to us in a special way to enable us to profess our (1) as strong and perfect (2) and (3) of Jesus Christ.
2. The (4) is the usual minister of Confirmation.
3. Christ instituted the Holy Eucharist at the (5).
4. The Holy Eucharist is a sacrament and a sacrifice; in it our Saviour, Jesus Christ, body and blood, soul and divinity, under the appearances of bread and wine is (6), (7), and (8).
5. By the appearances of bread and wine we mean their (9), (10), (11), and (12) and whatever else appears to the senses.
6. When our Lord said, "This is My body," the (13) was changed into His body; and when He said, "This is my blood," the (14) was changed into His blood.

1. (faith)
2. (Christians)
3. (soldiers)
4. (bishop)
5. (Last Supper)
6. (contained)
7. (offered)
8. (received)
9. (color)
10. (taste)
11. (weight)
12. (shape)
13. (bread)
14. (wine)

B. HOLY MASS: The Perfect Sacrifice (Text, *Living Like Christ, in Christ*, pp. 203–204)

PART I: Answer with YES or NO.

1. Does the altar stone contain relics of martyrs? — 1. Yes
2. Is the Credo an act of love? — 2. No
3. Is Christ the priest and victim in every Mass? — 3. Yes
4. Does Christ die again in the Mass? — 4. No
5. Is the Sacrifice of the Mass a perfect sacrifice? — 5. Yes
6. Were the sacrifices of the Old Testament perfect sacrifices? — 6. No
7. Do the prayers of the Ordinary of the Mass change from day to day? — 7. No
8. Do the Epistles contain the life of Christ? — 8. No
9. Is the Kyrie a plea for mercy? — 9. Yes
10. In the Collect do we tell God we are sorry for our sins? — 10. No

PART II: Choose the correct answer.

1. The Preface is an introduction to the: A. Offertory; *B. Consecration*; C. Sanctus.
2. The Sanctus is a prayer of: A. petition; *B. praise*; C. sorrow.
3. When the priest washes his fingers during Mass, he says the: A. Secret; *B. Lavabo*; C. Sanctus.
4. The sacrifices of the Old Testament are recalled: A. during the Offertory; B. just before the Consecration; *C. just after the Consecration*.
5. In the Kyrie, we honor the: A. martyrs; *B. Blessed Trinity*; C. apostles.
6. The Gloria is a prayer of: *A. praise*; B. petition; C. sorrow.
7. We partake of the Sacrificial Banquet at the: A. Offertory; *B. Communion*; C. Consecration.
8. The Confiteor is a prayer of: A. faith; B. praise; *C. sorrow*.
9. Christ's sacrifice on the cross was perfect because: A. God loved Christ; *B. the Priest and Victim were perfect*; C. Christ wanted to make the sacrifice.
10. In the Mass we offer ourselves to: *A. God*; B. all the saints; C. the Blessed Virgin.

PART III: Mark with an "O" the parts of the Mass which belong to the "Ordinary," and a "P" those which belong to the "Proper."

1. Confiteor	O		5. Introit	P
2. Epistle	P		6. Lavabo	O
3. Gloria	O		7. Collect	P
4. Kyrie	O		8. Credo	O

PART IV: Complete these sentences.

1. The Mass is the (1) of the New Law in which (2), through the priest, offers Himself to God in an unbloody manner under the appearances of (3) and (4).

1. (sacrifice)
2. (Christ)
3. (bread)
4. (wine)

2. The sacrifices of the Old Testament were not completely pleasing to God because the (5) and (6) were not perfect.
3. The bread and wine are changed into Christ's body and blood at the (7).
4. The offering of bread and wine represents the offering of the (8) along with the offering of (9).
5. The highest form of worship is the (10).

5. (priest)
6. (victim)
7. (consecration)
8. (faithful)
9. (Christ)
10. (Mass)

C. PENANCE — Temporal Punishment, Indulgences
(Text, *Living Like Christ, in Christ*, pp. 234–236)

TO PROVE MY MASTERY

PART I: Matching: Match each term in Column I with its meaning in Column II.

Column I
A. Absolution
B. Imperfect Contrition
C. Eternal punishment
D. Penance
E. Perfect contrition
F. Plenary Indulgence
G. Contrition
H. Sincere sorrow
I. Examination of conscience
J. Confessor
K. Venial sin
L. Temporal punishment

Column II
1. The prayers which the priest tells us to say as part of the punishment. (1) D
2. Punishment which lasts for a time. (2) L
3. The words and actions used by the priest when he forgives sins. (3) A
4. Remission of all temporal punishment due to sins. (4) F
5. Sorrow for sin. (5) G
6. Sorrow for sin because it offends a loving God. (6) E
7. The act of thinking back over how we have obeyed or disobeyed the Commandments of God and of the Church. (7) I
8. A less serious offense against the law of God. (8) K
9. Sorrow for sin because we fear the punishment of God. (9) B
10. True or real sorrow. (10) H

PART II: Answer with YES or NO.

1. Is having sorrow for our sins the most important part of the sacrament of Penance? 1. Yes
2. Must we be in the state of grace in order to gain an indulgence? 2. Yes
3. Is perfect contrition sorrow for sins because we have offended God whom we love? 3. Yes
4. Was the sacrament of Penance instituted at the Last Supper? 4. No
5. Should the sacrament of Penance be received only by those who have committed mortal sin? 5. No
6. May one who has not been baptized receive the sacrament of Penance? 6. No
7. Should we pray to the Holy Ghost for help in knowing our sins? 7. Yes
8. Does God forgive any sin which the priest forgives? 8. Yes
9. Must we say the penance which the priest gives us? 9. Yes
10. Does a plenary indulgence take away all temporal punishment due to our sins? 10. Yes

PART III: Choose the correct answer.

1. Christ instituted Penance on the feast of: A. Ascension; *B. Easter*; C. Pentecost.
2. The crucifix is usually seen in the confessional because; *A. it reminds us to be sorry for our sins*; B. it is a sacramental; C. it adds beauty to the confessional.
3. The most important part of confession is: A. perfect examination of conscience; B. firm resolution to sin no more; *C. true sorrow for our sins*.
4. We should go to confession often because: *A. we receive grace each time we go to confession*; B. it pleases our teacher; C. the Church tells us to.
5. A partial indulgence is the remission of: A. all; *B. part*; C. complete punishment due to our sins.
6. When the priest is giving us absolution we should: A. say the Act of Faith; B. say the Act of Love; *C. say the Act of Contrition*.
7. If we do not hear the penance which the priest gives us, we should: *A. ask the priest to repeat it*; B. say some prayers that we know well; C. say any prayer that we like.
8. If we cannot remember the exact number of times that we committed some sin we should: A. tell no number at all; *B. tell about how many times*; C. make up a number.
9. The remission of all the temporal punishment due to our sins is: A. a temporal indulgence; B. a partial indulgence; *C. a plenary indulgence*.
10. Contrition is: *A. the sincere sorrow for sin*; B. the desire to sin no more; C. the resolution to go to confession often.

PART IV: Matching beginnings and endings of sentences.

Beginnings:

1. We should receive the sacrament of Penance as often as possible (1) D
2. The sacrament of Penance is the sacrament (2) G
3. Our contrition is imperfect when we are sorry for our sins (3) H
4. After leaving the confessional, we should say our penance and (4) J
5. If we knowingly keep back a mortal sin, none of our sins are forgiven and (5) I
6. If we are truly sorry for our sins (6) C
7. If we know that a certain person, place, or thing will lead us into sin (7) E

8. By saying our penance we   (8) A
9. We should have contrition for venial sins   (9) B
10. Jesus instituted the sacrament of Penance   (10) F

Endings:

A. will shorten our purgatory.
B. because they too offend God and weaken our souls.
C. we will firmly resolve not to commit those sins again.
D. because each time we go to confession we receive special grace.
E. we must keep away from it.
F. because He is all merciful and wants us to go to heaven.
G. by which sins committed after Baptism are forgiven.
H. because we fear the punishments of God.
I. we have committed another mortal sin.
J. thank God for the grace He has given us.

D. EXTREME UNCTION — HOLY ORDERS — MATRIMONY (Text, *Living Like Christ, in Christ*, pp. 251–252).

TO PROVE MY MASTERY

PART I: Matching: Match each term in Column I with its meaning in Column II.

Column I	*Column II*
A. Sacraments of the living	1. Place of study for the priesthood. (1) C
B. Major Orders	2. Holy Communion received when one is in danger of death. (2) I
C. Seminary	3. The sacrament uniting a man and a woman for life. (3) G
D. Holy Orders	4. Last three steps in Holy Orders: subdeacon, deacon, and priest. (4) B
E. Nuptial Mass	5. Last anointing. (5) J
F. Religious vocation	6. Mass at which a special blessing is given the bride and groom. (6) E
G. Matrimony	7. Sacraments to be received in the state of grace. (7) A
H. Sacramental Grace	8. The sacrament through which a man becomes a priest. (8) D
I. Holy Viaticum	9. A call to serve God. (9) F
J. Extreme Unction	10. The special grace which each sacrament gives. (10) H

PART II: Complete the following.

1. We know from the epistle of (1) that Christ gave us the Sacrament of Extreme Unction.
2. We pray to (2) for the grace of a happy death.
3. Extreme Unction gives (3) and (4) to the soul and some-

   times to the (5).
4. In the Sacrament of Holy Orders the priest receives the power to offer the (6), to (7), and to administer the (8).
5. A priest is another (9) and for that reason should receive our greatest (10).
6. Holy Orders is a sacrament which is received only (11) because it leaves an (12) mark on the soul.
7. To become a priest a man must have good health, a good (13), and better than average (14).
8. The greatest gift the newly married couple can receive on their wedding day is (15).
9. The model for the Catholic home is the (16) and a good slogan for that home is (17).
10. A Catholic marriage takes place in Church and in the presence of a priest and (18).

1. (St. James)
2. (St. Joseph)
3. (health)
4. (strength)
5. (body)
6. (Mass)
7. (teach)
8. (sacraments)
9. (Christ)
10. (respect)
11. (once)
12. (indelible)
13. (character)
14. (intelligence)
15. (Christ in Holy Communion)
16. (Holy Family)
17. (The family that prays together, stays together)
18. (two witnesses)

PART III: Answer with YES or NO.

1. Was the Sacrament of Matrimony instituted in the Garden of Eden? — 1. No
2. May Extreme Unction be received only once? — 2. No
3. May Matrimony be received only once? — 3. No
4. May Holy Orders be received only once? — 4. Yes
5. May an infant receive the Sacrament of Extreme Unction? — 5. No
6. May an unconscious person receive the Sacrament of Extreme Unction? — 6. Yes
7. Does a priest have a greater power than any other living person? — 7. Yes
8. Were the apostles the first priests? — 8. Yes
9. May a Catholic be married before a Justice of the Peace? — 9. No
10. If a married man and woman do not get along, may they get a divorce and marry someone else? — 10. No

V. SUGGESTED ACTIVITIES

A. THE SEVEN SACRAMENTS

1. Read about your patron saint and prepare a short summary for the class.
2. Dramatize the administration of some of the sacraments.
3. Class renewal of the Baptismal Vows.
4. Compositions: What (fill in the name of the specific sacrament) means to me.
5. Original drawings of symbols of the sacraments.
6. Original filmstrips for the various sacraments.

7. Illustrated talks pertaining to the sacraments.
8. Learn or review hymns related to the sacraments:
Veni Creator
Adoro Te
Anima Christi
Ave Verum
O Sacrum Convivium
Pange Lingua

B. THE MASS, THE PERFECT SACRIFICE

1. Chart a time line showing acts of sacrifice from that of Abel in the Old Testament up to the Perfect Sacrifice in the New Testament.
2. Consult the liturgical calendar daily and report on the Mass for the day.
3. Set up a Mass Vocabulary on which all new terms encountered throughout the unit will be listed.
4. Set up a list of Latin words that have been learned during the study of the Mass. Have a contest matching them with their meanings.
5. Visit the church for the purpose of observing all symbolism. During an art period, discuss the symbolism which might be applied to the Mass. Follow the discussion with a lesson on drawing original symbols.
6. Study the Mass chants. Learn Mass XVI.
7. On a wall chart, arrange the parts of the Mass in their proper order.
8. Diagram the parts of the Mass. Place stickmen, standing, kneeling, or sitting as is proper at each of the particular parts of the Mass.
9. Prepare original Offertory and Communion Prayers. Use the Psalms if possible.
10. Locate information about the saints named in the Canon of the Mass.

VI. BIBLIOGRAPHY

A. THE SEVEN SACRAMENTS

FOR PUPILS:

Bandas, Rev. Rudolph G., and a School Sister of Notre Dame, *The Vine and the Branches;* Highway to Heaven Series, Book V (Milwaukee: Bruce Publishing Company, 1934).

Brennan, Rev. Gerald T., *Angel Food* (Milwaukee: Bruce Publishing Company, 1939).

——— *For Heaven's Sake* (Milwaukee: Bruce Publishing Company, 1942).

——— *Going His Way* (Milwaukee: Bruce Publishing Company, 1945).

Brother Ernest, *A Star Forever, The Story of St. Tarcisius* (Indiana: Dujarie Press, 1947).

Dennerle, Rev. George M., *Seven Wonder Gifts* (New York: Paulist Press, 1938).

Diamond, Rev. Wilfrid J., *Heavenwords* (Milwaukee: Bruce Publishing Company, 1947).

Dooley, Rev. Lester M., *Hello Halo!* (New York: Wagner, 1947).

Drees, Rev. Victor, *A Pictorial Explanation of the Seven Sacraments* (Cincinnati: St. Anthony Messenger, 1949).

Fitzgerald, Rev. John D., *Jolly Jacob and Other Stories* (Milwaukee: Bruce Publishing Company, 1946).

Fitzpatrick, Edward A., *The Life of the Soul;* Highway to Heaven Series, Book III (Milwaukee: Bruce Publishing Company, 1933).

Kelly, Rev. William R., *Our Sacraments* (New York: Benziger Brothers, Inc., 1927).

Kelly, Rev. William R., and Sister Mary Imelda, and Rev. M. A. Schumacher, *Living for God;* Living My Religion Series, Book IV (New York: Benziger Brothers, Inc., 1947).

——— *Living Through God's Gifts;* Living My Religion Series, Book V (New York: Benziger Brothers, Inc., 1947).

Pfeiffer, Rev. Harold A., *The Catholic Picture Dictionary* (New York: Catholic Manufacturing Company, 1948).

School Sister of Notre Dame, *Before Christ Came;* Highway to Heaven Series, Book IV (Milwaukee: Bruce Publishing Company, 1934).

Vacek, Joseph P., and Josephine Littel, *The Sacraments and the Mass* (St. Paul, Minn.: Catechetical Guild, 1939).

FOR TEACHERS:

Cavanagh, Rev. William J., *A Manual for Teachers of Religion* (Milwaukee: Bruce Publishing Company).

Fearon, Rev. John, *Graceful Living* (Westminster, Md.: The Newman Press, 1955).

Howell, Rev. Clifford, *Of Sacraments and Sacrifice* (Collegeville: The Liturgical Press, 1952).

Lahey, Rev. Thomas A., *The Children's Friend, A Life of Christ for Children* (St. Louis: B. Herder Book Company).

Roguet, Rev. A. M., *Christ Acts Through Sacraments* (Collegeville: The Liturgical Press).

Tonne, Rev. Arthur, *Talks on the Sacraments* (St. Louis: B. Herder Book Company).

Schumacher, Rev. M. A., *I Teach Catechism, Vols. II and III* (New York: Benziger Brothers, Inc., 1946).

Sister of Notre Dame, *Confirmation Stories* (St. Louis: B. Herder Book Company).

B. THE MASS

FOR PUPILS:

Bandas, Rev. Rudolph G., and a School Sister of Notre Dame, *The Vine and the Branches;* Highway to Heaven Series, Book V (Milwaukee: Bruce Publishing Company, 1934).

Beebe, Catherine and Robb Beebe, *We Know the Mass* (Paterson, N. J.: St. Anthony Guild Press, 1945).

Brogan, Rev. Edward P., and Mary J. Irwin, *A Missal for the Children's Mass* (Chicago: William H. Sadlier, Inc., 1949).

Bussard, Paul, *If I Be Lifted Up* (St. Paul, Minn.: The Catechetical Guild, 1944).

Dom Virgil Michel and Dom Basil Stegmann, *A Child of God;* Christ-Life Series in Religion, Book IV (New York: The Macmillan Company, 1935).

———— *The Redeeming Sacrifice;* Christ-Life Series in Religion, Book V (New York: The Macmillan Company, 1935).

Fitzpatrick, Edward A., *The Holy Sacrifice of the Mass;* Highway to Heaven Series, Book VI (Milwaukee: Bruce Publishing Company, 1936).

Horan, Ellamay, *The Holy Sacrifice of the Mass* (Chicago: W. H. Sadlier, Inc., 1948).

Kelly, Rev. William R., and Rev. Edmund J. Goebel, and Rev. M. A. Schumacher, *Living Through God's Gifts;* Living My Religion Series, Book V (New York: Benziger Brothers, Inc., 1947).

Kessler, Rev. William G., *Your Mass Visible* (Dubuque, Iowa: Allied Educational Service, 1942).

FOR TEACHERS:

Cavanagh, Rev. William J., *A Manual for Teachers of Religion* (Milwaukee: Bruce Publishing Company).

Frenway, Rev. Adolph D., *The Spirituality of the Mass* (St. Louis: B. Herder Book Company).

Gassner, Rev. Jerome, *The Canon of the Mass* (St. Louis: B. Herder Book Company).

Gihr, Rev. Nicholas, *The Holy Sacrifice of the Mass* (St. Louis: B. Herder Book Company).

Howell, Rev. Clifford, *Of Sacraments and Sacrifice* (Collegeville: The Liturgical Press, 1952).

Tonne, Rev. Arthur, *Talks on the Mass* (St. Louis: B. Herder Book Company).

VII. AUDIO-VISUAL AIDS

A. THE SEVEN SACRAMENTS

Illustrations: The Sacraments in Symbol (Collegeville: The Liturgical Press).

Illustrations: The Sacrament Teaching Cards (Maryknoll Sisters, Maryknoll, N. Y.

Illustrations: The Sacrament Teaching Cards (Maryknoll Sisters, Maryknoll, N. Y.).

Sound Filmstrip: Baptism and the New Creation (St. Paul: Catechetical Guild).

Sound Filmstrip: Sacraments in General; Each of the Sacraments individually. St. John's University, Brooklyn, N. Y. (New York: The Declan X. McMullen Company).

B. THE MASS

Illustrations: Chi-Rho Cards for Teaching the Mass (Maryknoll Sisters, Maryknoll, N. Y.).

Illustrations: Mass Photos (St. Paul: Catechetical Guild).

Illustrations: Mass Symbols, Rev. Godfrey Diekmann, O.S.B. (Collegeville: Liturgical Press).

Color Filmstrip. The Mass (St. Paul: Catechetical Guild).

Slides. The Mass (St. Paul: Catechetical Guild).

UNIT V. SACRAMENTALS AND PRAYER

(Text, *Living Like Christ, in Christ*, pp. 253–264)

I. OBJECTIVES

A. To develop an understanding of the sacramentals most commonly used by the Church.

B. To promote the reverential use of sacramentals.

C. To emphasize the value of the blessing attached to sacramentals.

D. To increase the understanding of prayer, lifting our minds and hearts to God.

E. To further the ability to pray with reverence and devotion.

II. TEACHER PRESENTATION OF UNIT V

The sacramentals should be presented in such a way that a love and respect for them is engendered and their use encouraged. At the same time any tendency toward a superstitious reliance on them is to be condemned.

In teaching prayer, gently lead the children to make their own acts of love, of contrition, of adoration. Let them know that their prayer can even be wordless, that prayer is a matter primarily of the mind and will. But also let it be known that our emotions and affections have a powerful role to play in life, even in prayer life. Stress that mere knowledge *about* prayer is not enough — what is desired is the act, prayer itself.

Give them oral examples in your own words of how to pray. For instance, after a lesson about God or any of His good deeds to us, you might conclude: "We have learned much today about how great God is and how much He has done to show His love for us. Should we now go over to church, kneel, and say to our Blessed Lord, 'Jesus, my God, You are great and good and mighty and holy. I adore You, I thank You for having done so much for me. I am sorry for every sin I have ever committed. Give me Your grace to be a good Catholic. Help me bring others to You and Your Church.'"

Help the children to realize what the presence of God means and try to get them to live ever in God's presence: praying, playing, studying, working — yes, and even sleeping in the awareness that we are in His presence and that He dwells within us.

III. OUTLINE OF SUBJECT MATTER FOR UNIT V

CHAPTER 26. Sacramentals: Another Means of Grace

I. Sacramentals, another means of grace

A. What sacramentals are:
   1. Holy things or actions
   2. Must be used or performed in a holy way

B. Sacramentals most commonly used:
   1. Holy water
   2. Blessed candles
   3. Crucifixes
   4. Images of our Lord
   5. Images of saints
   6. Medals
   7. Rosaries
   8. The Sign of the Cross

C. Effect of Sacramentals:
   1. Take away venial sin
   2. Obtain grace
   3. Remit temporal punishment
   4. Protect us against evil spirits and temptations

CHAPTER 27. Prayer: Lifting Our Minds and Hearts to God

I. Prayer, another means of grace

A. What prayer is:
   1. Lifting our minds and hearts to God in word
   2. Lifting our minds and hearts to God in thought

B. Why we pray:
   1. To adore God
   2. To thank God
   3. To obtain pardon from God
   4. To ask graces for ourselves and others

C. For whom we should pray:
   1. Ourselves
   2. Parents, relatives
   3. Friends, enemies, sinners
   4. Souls in purgatory
   5. Pope, bishops, priests of the Church
   6. Officials of country

D. How we should pray:
1. With proper intention
2. With faith and reverence
3. In our own words or thoughts
4. Use prayer books

IV. ANSWER KEY TO END-UNIT TESTS IN TEXTBOOK

SACRAMENTALS AND PRAYERS (Text, *Living Like Christ, in Christ*, p. 264)

TO PROVE MY MASTERY

PART I: Choose the correct answer.

1. Sacramentals were instituted by: A. Christ; *B. the Church;*   C. a Saint.
2. Sacramentals take away: *A. venial sin;*   B. original sin;   C. mortal sin.
3. The best prayer is: A. The Apostles' Creed; *B. The Our Father;*   C. The Hail Mary.
4. Our greatest model for prayer is: A. St. Peter; B. our patron saint;   *C. Christ.*
5. Sacramentals: *A. provide means of grace;*   B. give sanctifying grace;   C. give grace by themselves.
6. Prayer: A. must always be said aloud;   *B. is necessary for salvation;*   C. should be read from a book.

PART II: Matching: Match each term in Column I with its meaning in Column II.

Column I	*Column II*
A. Sacramentals	1. the best prayer (1) **D**
B. Prayer	2. temporal favor (2) **G**
C. Sign of the Cross	3. a prayer and a sacramental (3) **C**
D. The Our Father	
E. Blessed Trinity	4. highest form of prayer (4) **H**
F. Holy Water	
G. Health	5. important mystery of our religion (5) **E**
H. Adoration	6. blessed objects (6) **A**
I. Grace	7. gift of God (7) **I**
	8. talking with God (8) **B**
	9. a sacramental (9) **F**

PART III: Answer the following.

1. Name four sacramentals that you use most frequently.   (holy water; candles; ashes; palms; crucifixes; medals; etc.)
2. Tell the four reasons why we pray.   (to adore God; to thank God; to obtain pardon for sin; to ask for graces and blessings)
3. Name two mysteries expressed by the Sign of the Cross.   (the Unity of God; the Trinity; the Redemption)

V. SUGGESTED ACTIVITIES

1. Reports on the difference between sacraments and sacramentals.
2. Compositions explaining the value of specific sacramentals.
3. Dramatizations which stress the correct use of sacramentals.
4. Original drawings of various sacramentals.
5. Vocabulary chart including new words and terms learned in this study.
6. Prepare reports or compositions about the origin of our common prayers.
7. Make a "Class Raccolta" of common indulgenced ejaculations. Memorize ten of them.
8. Illustrate the four purposes of prayer.
9. Prepare a filmstrip showing the various persons for whom we should pray.

VI. BIBLIOGRAPHY

FOR PUPILS:

Bandas, Rev. Rudolph G., and a School Sister of Notre Dame, *The Vine and the Branches;* Highway to Heaven Series, Book V (Milwaukee: Bruce Publishing Company, 1934).

Brennan, Rev. Gerald T., *For Heaven's Sake* (Milwaukee: Bruce Publishing Company, 1942).

———— *Going His Way* (Milwaukee: Bruce Publishing Company, 1945).

Cook, Frederick, *Child With Folded Hands* (Paterson, N. J.: St. Anthony Guild Press, 1941).

Diamond, Rev. Wilfrid J., *Heavenwords* (Milwaukee: Bruce Publishing Company, 1947).

Dooley, Rev. Lester M., *Hello Halo!* (New York: Wagner, 1947).

Fitzpatrick, Edward A., *The Life of the Soul;* Highway to Heaven Series, Book III (Milwaukee: Bruce Publishing Company, 1933).

———— *The Highway to God;* Highway to Heaven Series, Books VII–VIII (Milwaukee: Bruce Publishing Company, 1933).

Gasparri, Peter Cardinal, *Catholic Faith, Book II* (New York: P. J. Kenedy and Sons, 1939).

Kelly, Rev. William R., and Sister Mary Imelda, and Rev. M. A. Schumacher, *Living Through God's Gifts;* Living My Religion Series, Book V (New York: Benziger Brothers, Inc., 1947).

Kelly, Rev. William R., and Sister Mary Imelda, and Rev. Edmund Goebel, and Rev. Daniel M. Dougherty, *Living in God's Church;* Living My Religion Series, Book VI (New York: Benziger Brothers, Inc., 1948).

———— *Living for Triumph;* Living My Religion Series, Book VII (New York: Benziger Brothers, Inc., 1949).

Lord, Daniel A., *The Rosary* (New York: William J. Hirten Company, 1943).

Pfeiffer, Rev. Harold A., *The Catholic Picture Dictionary* (New York: Catholic Manufacturing Company, 1948).

School Sister of Notre Dame, *Before Christ Came; Highway to Heaven Series*, Book IV (Milwaukee: Bruce Publishing Company, 1934).

Sister Mary Jean Dorcy, *Our Lady's Feasts* (New York: Sheed and Ward, 1945).

Strugnell, Rev. Joseph, *When Ye Pray, Pray Ye Thus* (Paterson, N. J.: St. Anthony Guild Press, 1943).

FOR TEACHERS:

Broderick, Robert C., *The Catholic Concise Encyclopedia* (St. Paul: Catechetical Guild, 1957).

Cavanagh, Rev. William J., *A Manual for Teachers of Religion* (Milwaukee: Bruce Publishing Company).

Lahey, Rev. Thomas A., *The Children's Friend, A Life of Christ for Children* (St. Louis: B. Herder Book Company).

Lovasik, Rev. Lawrence G., *The Catholic Picture Bible* (New York: Catholic Book Publishing Company).

——— *Catechism in Stories* (Milwaukee: Bruce Publishing Company).

Mueller, Dr. Therese, *Our Children's Year of Grace* (Collegeville: The Liturgical Press).

Parsch, Rev. Pius, *The Church's Year of Grace* in Five Volumes (Collegeville: The Liturgical Press).

Schumacher, Rev. M. A., *I Teach Catechism*, Vols. II and III (New York: Benziger Brothers, Inc., 1946).

Sister Joanne, S.N.D., *The Story of Redemption for Children* (Collegeville: Liturgical Press).

——— *Mysteries of the Rosary for the Family* (Collegeville: Liturgical Press).

VII. AUDIO-VISUAL AIDS

Illustrations: Symbols for Feasts and Commons. Clemens Schmidt (Collegeville: Liturgical Press).

Illustrations: Station Cards. Clemens Schmidt (Collegeville: Liturgical Press).

Illustrations: The Rosary (St. Paul: Catechetical Guild).

Illustrations: Externals of the Liturgy (St. Paul: Catechetical Guild).

Prayer Chart (St. Paul: Catechetical Guild).

Color Filmstrips: Stations of the Cross; Mysteries of the Rosary; Fishers of Men (Vocation film); St. John Vianney (Vocation film).

Sound Filmstrip: Sacramentals; Prayer. St. John's University, Brooklyn, N. Y. (New York: The Declan X. McMullen Company).